SUCCESS IN MINISTRY

Bob Hankins

Success in Ministry

Lessons from a Spiritual Father

WestBow
PRESS®
A DIVISION OF THOMAS NELSON
& ZONDERVAN

This book is a work of non-fiction. Unless otherwise noted, the author and the publisher make no explicit guarantees as to the accuracy of the information contained in this book and in some cases, names of people and places have been altered to protect their privacy.

Scripture taken from the King James Version of the Bible.

WestBow Press books may be ordered through booksellers or by contacting:

WestBow Press
A Division of Thomas Nelson & Zondervan
1663 Liberty Drive
Bloomington, IN 47403
www.westbowpress.com
1 (866) 928-1240

Because of the dynamic nature of the Internet, any web addresses or links contained in this book may have changed since publication and may no longer be valid. The views expressed in this work are solely those of the author and do not necessarily reflect the views of the publisher, and the publisher hereby disclaims any responsibility for them.

Any people depicted in stock imagery provided by Thinkstock are models, and such images are being used for illustrative purposes only.
Certain stock imagery © Thinkstock.

ISBN: 978-1-5127-2972-6 (sc)
ISBN: 978-1-5127-2969-6 (e)

Library of Congress Control Number: 2016901701

Print information available on the last page.

WestBow Press rev. date: 03/11/2016

Biography of B. B. Hankins and Velma Hankins

B. B. Hankins was the pastor of the Gulf Coast Christian Center in West Columbia, Texas, for forty-nine years and was in pastoral ministry for fifty-five years. He earned a bachelor's degree from Southwestern University in Waxahachie, Texas. It was at college that he met his wife, Velma Dawes, and they were married in 1947.

Velma's parents were Bedford and Mae Dawes, and they were from Pawhuska, Oklahoma. Velma had one sister, Sarah Dawes, and one brother, Lee Dawes. B. B.'s parents were the Reverend Robert and Rachel Muirhead Hankins, who are mentioned several times in this book. They planted a church in the community of Bethel, right outside Fairfield, Texas. The original church building at Bethel has been restored and is on display at the Freestone County Historical Museum in Fairfield. My aunt, Jean Hankins Kelley, took the initiative and paid for most of the expense of moving and restoring the building. My father had two sisters, Sue Hankins Garrick and Jean Hankins Kelley, who loved and supported him.

B. B. Hankins pastored his first church in Grapeland, Texas, at age twenty. He also pastored in Flynn, Texas, before moving to West Columbia in 1954. The Gulf Coast Christian Center began in an old wooden building on Bernard Street and grew to be one of the largest churches in the Assemblies of God fellowship in the 1980s. In 1987, the church's Sunday school enrollment was 1,400 people, with an average worship attendance of 950 in a town of 4,500 people. Many well-known ministers have ministered at the Gulf Coast Christian

Center over the years. They include John Osteen, Joyce Meyer, Kenneth Copeland, Kenneth Hagin, and Jesse Duplantis.

B. B. Hankins had an impact on the city of West Columbia and was instrumental in founding the Christian Senior Citizen's Center, which provides daily hot meals and activities for senior citizens, and Columbia Christian School, which offered a Christian educational environment for families in the Brazoria County area for close to twenty years before closing in 2007. Pastor Hankins's community service included serving as president and director of the West Columbia Rotary Club, director of the West Columbia Chamber of Commerce, chairman of the First Capital Bicentennial Committee, and chaplain of the West Columbia Volunteer Fire Department. He was named Man of the Year by the West Columbia Chamber of Commerce in 1976.

B. B. Hankins's greatest legacy, however, is the ministers and spiritual sons and daughters who have come out of the Gulf Coast Christian Center and established churches and ministries all over the world. Thirty spiritual sons and daughters who were trained at the Gulf Coast Christian Center during B. B. Hankins's tenure are in vocational ministry today. There are many examples of how the ministry of B. B. and Velma Hankins has touched the world through their spiritual sons and daughters. A Bible college and Christian school in the Congo was established by one of their spiritual sons. A church was built in Thailand and is pastored by former members of the Gulf Coast Christian Center. B. B. Hankins always said that you can get anywhere in the world from West Columbia.

The Hankins children were all called to vocational ministry as well. The oldest son, Mike Hankins, is pastor of Church in the City in Rowlett, Texas. Mark Hankins is an evangelist who ministers all over the world, and daughter Faith Hankins was a pastor's wife for many years and an accomplished worship leader. Bob served as the associate pastor under his father for four years and then became senior pastor of the Gulf Coast Christian Center in 2003. The Hankinses have twelve grandchildren, of whom eight to date have followed in their grandparents' footsteps in vocational ministry. The Hankinses' granddaughters Christian Hankins and Annie Stanford serve in churches in Australia. Listed in order by age, the grandchildren are Julie Hankins Wood, Lyndi Hankins Rohde, Aaron Hankins, Ryan Hankins, Alicia Hankins Moran, Kynsie Hankins Zakem, Robert Wood, Christian Hankins, Geoffrey Wood, Annie Hankins Stanford, Audrea Wood Garcia, and Lauren Wood.

Contents

FOREWORD

Get ready! The book you are holding in your hands right now has the power to change your life forever. How can I say that with such boldness and confidence? Because the people this book is about did just that for me.

Some of you who are reading this are already aware of B. B. and Velma Hankins and the trails that they blazed by faith. But for those of you who are not, it is my greatest honor and pleasure to introduce you to two of the finest people who I have ever had the privilege of knowing.

When I think about B. B. and Velma Hankins and reflect on their life and ministry, I think of nothing but integrity, character, and a desire to do the will of God. To say that they had passion and vision would be an understatement. They started a church in the small town of West Columbia, Texas, and it grew to be one of the largest in their area. People love success, and B. B. and Velma were the definition of success in a very small place. To know them was to love them, and B. B. was Dad to just about everybody in that town.

Everything they did was amazing, and they left an indelible mark on the lives of countless people and nations. Their legacy lives not only through their children and grandchildren (most of whom are in full-time ministry today) but also through the many spiritual sons and daughters they have raised up, of whom I am one. Little did I realize when I met them many years ago that they would change my life forever and for the better. I am eternally grateful for their influence on my life, and I pray that as you read this book, their words, their wisdom, and the spirit of who they were will influence you as well.

This book will illuminate your thinking, illuminate your vision, and improve your character and understanding of the Word of God. Although they are both in heaven today, B. B.'s and Velma's words and teachings are still as profound and practical today as they were when they were first preached. I personally believe that these words will last until Jesus comes again.

Enjoy this book, because I certainly did.

Dr. Jesse Duplantis

ACKNOWLEDGMENTS

I want to acknowledge all those who have helped in writing this book. Sue Laird, Tracy Leavell, Carolyn Chafin, Christian Hankins, and Candy Hankins have helped transcribe the tapes of my father's teaching. I also want to acknowledge Suzanne Mullins, who was my father's faithful employee for twenty-one years before he went to be with Jesus. My wife, Candy, and my daughters, Christian and Annie, lovingly cared for my mother during the last years of her life.

I can't forget those faithful members of the Gulf Coast Christian Center who began attending the church in the 1960s and were loyal to my father for more than forty years. Some of them passed to heaven prior to the writing of this book, and others are still attending the church today. Some of the names are Oyce Woolems, Clive Rush, Milton and Anice Fenley, Evelyn Stump and her son David, Sydney and Reba Smith, Maxine Stewart, Dianne Reynolds, James Mitchell, Jeff and Jo Ann Roe, David Roe, Ella Barnett, Chuck and Winona Sherrill and Pati Webb.

Most of all, I want to acknowledge my mother, Velma Hankins. She went to her eternal reward in 2008 and is greatly missed by the many people whose lives she influenced. This book contains mainly my father's teaching, but I've included three chapters of my mother's teaching. She was his faithful partner in ministry for fifty-five years. Her prayers, support, and dedication to his life were instrumental in his success. Velma was a spiritual mother to many sons and daughters and a great woman of God. This book is a tribute to her life as well as his.

INTRODUCTION

In November 2002, my father was a patient at Triumph Hospital in Sugar Land, Texas. He was recovering from a stroke, and we would try to communicate with him by reading his lips. One evening when I was visiting him, he motioned with his hands that he wanted to write. I gave him a pen and a pad, and he tried to write a message. He wasn't able to write anything legible, because of the condition that the stroke had left him in. During another visit around that time, he again tried to write and move his lips to get a message to me, but again I wasn't able to understand what he was trying to say. In December, my father's condition grew worse, and he was unable to communicate. Our family and church members continued to faithfully visit my father daily during his illness.

On January 16, 2003, I received a phone call around nine o'clock at night from my sister, Faith Hankins. She was at the hospital, and my father was not expected to live through the night. I picked my mother up from her home and rushed the fifty miles to Sugar Land as quickly as I could. When we arrived in my father's room, he had already gone to be with Jesus. Tears rushed down our faces as we got to be with my father's body for the last time. As I walked out of the hospital, it suddenly dawned on me what my father was trying to tell me. He wanted me to write the book that he had always intended to write. I was my father's associate pastor for four years, and we had talked several times about him writing a book. I had offered to help him write it. I know that he intended to write a book but never had the opportunity. So I am writing it for him to honor him. I want people to remember what a great man he was, but even more importantly, the truths that he learned about pastoral ministry need to be passed on to the next generation.

My father hosted a Spiritual Sons Conference for eleven years in West Columbia, Texas. It was a three-day meeting in which he would teach principles of ministry to his spiritual sons. The spiritual sons were ministers who had connected with my father during Dad's forty-nine years of ministry in West Columbia. Some had grown up in his church, and others had connected with him throughout the years. As of 2015, there are thirty spiritual sons and daughters in vocational ministry who were raised in the Gulf Coast Christian Center during his forty-nine years as pastor of the church. Those thirty sons and daughters have sixteen children who are in vocational ministry. This book is compiled from the recordings of the spiritual sons meetings, along with some of my dad's sermons and my mother's teachings for women. I also added some of my own content in some messages to fill out a chapter.

My prayer is that this book will be a blessing to Christians and ministers for many years to come.

Bob Hankins

PHOTOGRAPHS

B.B. Hankins

B.B. and Velma Hankins

B.B. and Velma Hankins with their spiritual sons and daughters in 1999

Bob and Candy Hankins, Christian Hankins and Tim and Annie Stanford at the wedding of Tim and Annie Stanford in 2014

The extended Hankins family at the wedding of Will and Audrea Garcia in 2013

Robert Hankins, B.B. Hankins' father

Chapter 1

MY VISION FOR THE SPIRITUAL SONS

You can get anywhere in the world from here.

—B. B. Hankins

Whenever I teach from an Old Testament text, I always ask myself, "How does this relate to the New Testament?" We need to be able to connect the Old and the New Testaments together.

Joel 2:28 says, "And it shall come to pass afterward, that I will pour out my spirit upon all flesh; and your sons and daughters shall prophesy, your old men shall dream dreams, and your young men shall see visions."

Peter stood up on the day of Pentecost in Acts chapter 2 and said the same thing. He stood up and answered the questions of those who were honest doubters. Peter said, "This is that which was spoken by the prophet Joel."

In the new covenant, every believer can be filled with the Holy Spirit. God pours out his Spirit on hungry people. If we have a self-satisfied church, there won't be much happening spiritually. Jesus went into the highways and hedges and went after needy people. The Bible says, "Where there is no vision, the people perish."

I went with my father, Robert Hankins, when I was a boy to hear him preach in different churches. I was exposed to the gospel and what God was doing. Sometimes children are never in Holy Spirit–inspired services, but I saw the Holy Spirit moving when I was a child. I had the privilege of being mentored by my father until I was twenty-six years old. He came to West Columbia and preached one time before he passed away. My mother told me later that he said, "That church was one of the hardest places I ever preached in."

My father was a pioneering pastor, and he began by going out on weekends and preaching while he worked a job in Dallas. He went to a night Bible school for young men who needed training. When he got licensed with the Assemblies of God, they told him that they didn't have any churches; if he wanted a church, he would have to go out and start one.

The first church he had, he started himself. That is the ideal situation if you want to have a spirit of cooperation in your church and you want the people to have the vision that *you* have.

My father had a world missions vision that was always part of our lives. Many missionaries stayed at our house. In those days it was standard procedure for the evangelist or missionary to stay in homes. I was around people with dedication and commitment. We had Bible school students who would come and stay with us and work in the church.

My dad had very little concern about material things, and he didn't leave us any material goods when he died. What he left me was faith in God, and when you have that, you don't need anyone to leave you anything else. He did teach me how to work, and that is important. The ministry is work, and if you aren't diligent in doing other things, you won't be successful in ministry.

My dad had an old car when he pastored the First Assembly of God in Fairfield, and he had saved $1,000 to buy a new one. In those days you could buy a new car for $2,000. We had a missions convention at the church, and my dad gave away the $1,000 he had saved. My sisters and I were disappointed because we were looking forward to having a new car. In a few months a man gave my dad an almost new car that was nicer than the one he would have purchased.

My father never had the opportunity to minister overseas, but he was a home missionary. He started two churches and birthed them by the Holy Spirit. He never got to go overseas, but in my lifetime my wife and I have been many places overseas to preach the gospel. Our church here in West Columbia has sent out many home and foreign missionaries.

My father was a man of prayer and the Word. He believed in preaching the Word. He would always tell me, "Son, preach the Word." He believed that the preaching of the Word should be first priority. He was telling me that I should preach the Word and not my own ideas. He also told me to learn how to be a good preacher so I could feed the people.

If you study and pray and prepare to preach for a service and God doesn't give you something to say, it means that God is going to do something different in the service. God expects us to prepare, and you need to learn how to preach. It is important to be able to teach the Word of God. Many of the early Pentecostal preachers were self-taught preachers. They learned how to be strong preachers of the Word without formal training. They weren't uneducated because they had never been to Bible college. Education can be a strong advantage, and God doesn't promote ignorance. If we don't have the opportunity for a formal education, then we have to educate ourselves.

We are imparting vision all the time to the people we work with and associate with. I always liked to have older ministers come and preach for me. These seasoned ministers blessed the church, but I also learned from them by relationships. I recently had Roy Hicks at the church, and I enjoyed talking with him for several hours about the things of God. This Spiritual Sons group began by the Spirit because I didn't try to start it. I had ministers come here seeking a spiritual father, and I was asked to minister at other churches, where the pastors would seek counsel. We started having a short session during Camp Meeting, and then I decided to have a longer meeting during September.

The mission of the church will always remain the same. Jesus said, "Go into all the world and preach the gospel to every creature." We also have the instructions from the apostle Paul on how to build the church. No ministry will last that was not founded by its involvement with a local church. I am addressing parachurch organizations. Many of them have no relationship with a local church. Even parachurch organizations should be part of a local church.

Some of my dreams of the Spirit are first of all for my own personal family to do the will of God. The first priority in your vision should be for your family. Your second priority in your vision should be to build a strong church. Strong churches can reach the community and the world. Strong churches have the power to establish families in the kingdom of God.

Some people say, "I want our church to stay small." Some people want to go to a church where they can be comfortable. What they are really saying is "Let the rest of the world go to hell." There should be a desire in the hearts of Christians to reach out to others. If we have that, we are going to reach out, and we are going to grow.

One of my dreams is to put into writing at least some of the things that I have learned from the Lord in my lifetime. I have been in the ministry almost all my life. I was five years old when my dad started preaching. I started pastoring my first church in 1948.

My dream is to touch the people of the nations. God will give us the heathen for our inheritance.

I love to go back to the places where my father pastored. The people there love me dearly because of him. One of my father's converts was a bootlegger named Albert Finch. He told me, "My family was in a mess when your father came down to Fairfield to preach the gospel." That is an inheritance. Our vision has to be a world vision.

My dream is that this Spiritual Sons group can join together to impact cities and nations for God. My dream includes the poor, the sick, and the homeless. God has given me divine appointments with people of other nations. I have begun, but now you are going to have to finish the vision. There is much to be done that I cannot do and won't live long enough to do. I want to minister to you so that you can fulfill your vision. If we carry out our dream, what God can do through us is unlimited.

Chapter 2
GRACE FOR RELATIONSHIPS

You will either get bitter or you will get better.
—B. B. Hankins

Hebrews 6:13–18 says, "For when God made a promise to Abraham, because he could swear by no one greater, He swore by himself ... that by two immutable things, in which it is impossible for God to lie, we might have strong consolation, who have fled for refuge to lay hold of the hope set before us."

I used to wonder what the two immutable things were that are talked about in verse 18. They are the promise itself and the impossibility for God to lie. God has been a covenant God ever since the beginning. This is like a contract and money-back guarantee given by the seller. If God said it, I believe it, and that settles it. The gift of Jesus Christ is God's guarantee of covenant relationship with us. God has given us grace to be in covenant with him.

Once a friend of mine, who was a pastor, had a nervous breakdown. He ended up in a mental hospital. I was talking to him after he was released, and he asked me, "How do you put up with these people?" I told him that even though people have faults, thank God they are still in the race. My friend was too hard on other people and himself. The church is a family and not a business.

A family is supposed to have long-term relationships and tolerance for each other. All of us have had many opportunities to be derailed, but thank God for his grace. We had people around us who prayed for us and loved us, and we made it. There have been times in pastoring this church that we were so close to failure. I knew that it was through much prayer and the grace of God that we persevered. New challenges to your ministry arise every week. I'm thankful that we have a God who answers prayer. When a challenge faced me, I would pray, and then I would stay in faith.

The hardest part is to stay in faith after you have prayed. The best way to deal with worry and anxiety over problems and challenges is to praise God for the answer instead of thinking and talking defeat. That is not always easy to do, but it works. I ask God for the answer once, and then I begin to thank him for the answer. I know that the devil works against ministers by magnifying problems and trying to get you into fear. Fear is always defeated by faith.

It takes the grace of God to maintain relationships with people, because there are always hurdles that have to be overcome. Anytime you get two or more people together, you will have conflicts. Conflicts aren't fun but sometimes they are necessary. If people would practice biblical conflict resolution according to Matthew chapter 18, we would have a lot fewer problems in the church.

Matthew 18:15 says, "If your brother trespasses against you, go and tell him his fault between you and him alone." The key word in this verse is *alone*. If people are offended, they tell everyone else except the one who offended them. They tell everyone else either because they don't have the courage to confront someone or because they are hoping to get other people on their side. I've learned that there are two sides to every story, and the only way that you can know the truth is to get both parties together and hear both sides. People tend to tell about their conflicts with others in ways that benefit them. You can hear one person tell you what someone else has done to them and get angry with the other person.

What they told you in most cases was just part of the truth. This isn't just for church members; it is for pastors too. As pastors we can watch people do things that irritate us and need to be corrected and not have the courage to confront those people. We can stay irritated for a long time or, even worse, tell everyone else in the church about it.

The challenge is having the wisdom to know what needs to be corrected and what can be overlooked. If people come to me in the right spirit and tell me something that needs to be corrected in my ministry or the church, I will listen to them. However, when they criticize me or the church to others, especially in a destructive way, it causes me to get angry. A pastor also has to be careful that he doesn't criticize his church members in a destructive way.

A pastor has to have discretion in what he communicates to others. You don't have to tell everyone you know about everything you know. I don't criticize other pastors or other churches so that people will come to my church. Even if I know something negative about another church or pastor, I don't talk to others about it unless there is a biblical reason to do so.

A minister's first duty is to please God. He has to lead the church according to the Word of God. The Word of God is the guide for any issues that arise in the church. If there is ever a conflict between pleasing God and pleasing other people, you had better choose God. I have found that God is my source and not people.

It seems as if I have pastored half of the people in Brazoria County at one time or another. People come and people go, but God is my source. I have learned not to be bitter when people leave my church because sometimes it is a blessing in disguise. If someone is disgruntled with the church or me and we can't work it out, then it is best for me and for them that they leave. They can leave more easily than I can, because I would have to move, and they only have to change churches. I know that my ministry is not for everyone, even though I would like it to be. I'm not going to sow bad seed by walking in bitterness or reacting to what others have said about me. If someone else is sowing bad seed then their harvest will come back to them.

My friend Arthur Locke used to say, "People will send you off talking to yourself." They will, unless you practice forgiveness and walking in love. The best way to forgive someone is to stop talking about him or her. Every time you talk about a grievance, you plant a little more hurt and anger in your heart. Instead of talking about what they did, begin to say, "I forgive them in the name of Jesus." Then pray that God will help them and bless them. In time you will be able to let go of offenses.

I heard a radio preacher say, "I'm not here by being careful, but I am here by the grace of God." Grace is the undeserved favor of God. James 4:6 says, "He gives more grace." God gives us grace to overcome in our ministry assignment. He gives us grace to be in relationship with people. First we have to know that we are called by God to be in the place we are. When we know we are called by God it settles any other issues or disappointments that may arise. Thank God that he will supply the grace that you need if you'll ask him for it.

Chapter 3

SEASONS OF THE SPIRIT

The anointing of the Holy Spirit will cause you to see your divine purpose.

—B. B. Hankins

Pentecost began with a prayer meeting, and when the Spirit moved in Topeka, Kansas, in the early 1900s, it was on a group of students in a prayer meeting. The Azusa Street revival began with people who were hungry for God, who came to seek God and pray.

I believe that we can plan revival. If we are halfhearted in our preparation for revival, then God can't move the way he wants to in our churches. The only hope for America is for the church to be revived. Political parties and politicians won't be able to save our nation.

How can we plan for revival? You can get a good speaker and advertise, but that is not enough. When I was a boy, we would continue a revival until we had a breakthrough. We used to have extended meetings. I have had many extended revivals in my church here.

For the revival to be successful, it has to be under the direction of the Holy Spirit. The biblical pattern for revival is found in the Feasts of the Old Testament. When God established the seven Feasts of the nation of Israel, he communicated an element of his plan. Each feast was celebrated in the yearly calendar. In each feast a theme was emphasized to the nation of Israel. The Passover reminded them of how God had delivered them from bondage.

Each feast had a spiritual truth that was a reminder to them every year, and these events were revisited every year. We have to be reminded of God's truth each year. In Jesus's day, the Feast of Pentecost was a celebration of the giving of the Law on Mount Sinai. When the Holy Spirit fell on the day of Pentecost, God was fulfilling his promise to Israel. He had promised to make a new covenant with them. God put his law in their hearts as was prophesied by the prophet Jeremiah. In the Upper Room, 120 people were changed by the power of the Holy Spirit. On the day of Pentecost the church was born and began to change the world. Jesus fulfilled the Feasts in his death, burial, and resurrection.

As ministers, we can emphasize these special days that teach spiritual truths. We need to see these special days filled with a substance of spiritual reality rather than just a program that we follow each year.

Twenty years after Jesus's resurrection, the apostle Paul had a strong desire to be in Jerusalem for the celebration of Pentecost. I know that it was much more than just a ceremony. I believe Paul wanted to be there because the move of the Holy Spirit was still real.

Pentecostals should make the day of Pentecost our biggest celebration. Some charismatics reject all liturgical forms by saying, "We don't want to be dead," but we can let the Holy Spirit make special days real in us so that we can have revival all year long. We can preach on the Holy Spirit from Easter until Pentecost. I believe something would break out in our churches if we did. There is a biblical and theological foundation for our Pentecostal practices. You can't build a spiritual life or a church on a one-time experience. People need a scriptural basis for their experiences.

When I was a boy in church, I saw people do crazy things in services when the Holy Spirit was moving that I didn't like. When I was sixteen, I got out the Bible in my bedroom and searched the Scriptures to see if the manifestations of the Holy Spirit were in the

Bible. That was the thing that kept me from leaving the Pentecostals and going to another denomination.

Every time I go to Israel, I go to the Upper Room. It's not the same Upper Room that the disciples were in, but it is close to the same place. The last time I went to the Upper Room, Pastor Bob Nichols preached, and people were baptized in the Holy Spirit in that Upper Room. God still confirms his Word with signs following. God wants to move today with the same power that he demonstrated in the New Testament.

If we want a "move of the Holy Spirit," then we are the ones who have to move. God never changes, and he never moves. A "move of God" happens when people start to move closer to God. The problem is that many Christians aren't very hungry for the things of God. They are distracted by the activities of life and are satisfied with the spiritual status quo.

I've seen many people come back to God when they need a job. If they are out of work, they start coming to church and serving God and praying for a job. Then God helps them find a good job, and they drop out of church and stop serving him. They didn't really want a relationship with God; they just wanted a job. If they would be dedicated and serve God continually, they wouldn't end up in financial jams. They don't know that God is their source and their heavenly Father. God sent the Holy Spirit to provide us with more than just a job. Jesus said that we would be empowered by the Holy Spirit to fulfill the Great Commission.

It is the wind of the Holy Spirit that brings life to a church or a nation. In Ezekiel chapter 37, the Holy Spirit took Ezekiel to a valley of dry bones. Ezekiel said that the bones were very dry. That is the condition of the church in America today, and it may be the condition of your church.

God told Ezekiel to prophesy to the bones and command them to hear the Word of the Lord. We can prophesy to the church in America and command her to hear the Word of the Lord. You can prophesy to your dead and dry church and command it to hear the Word of the Lord.

Ezekiel prophesied to the wind and said, "Breathe upon these dead that they may live"; breath came into them, and they came to life. Jesus used the wind as a metaphor for the Holy Spirit. It is the wind of the Spirit that causes life to enter into dry bones.

It is amazing how a cool wind can change a stagnant atmosphere. I live in South Texas where summer begins in May and ends in October. The summers are unbearably hot and humid. Sometime around the first of October we get our first cool front. A cool front is just a north wind that blows in. The north wind drives out the humidity and makes the atmosphere enjoyable again.

On the day of Pentecost the people heard a sound like a rushing, mighty wind. The wind began to blow, and a group of defeated disciples were totally transformed. God said that he would "pour out his spirit on all flesh in the last days." The last days began on the day of Pentecost, and we are still in the last days. Pentecost happens when people get hungry enough to ask for the wind of the Spirit to blow on them.

Chapter 4

THE IMPORTANCE OF PRAYER IN MINISTRY

The poorest person in the world is someone who doesn't have anyone praying for them.

—B. B. Hankins

Jesus told his disciples in John 15:4 that they had to abide in him to bear fruit. To abide with someone is to live with them and have a relationship with them. It's impossible to have a relationship with someone unless you spend time communicating with them.

Our relationship time with Jesus is our prayer life. I look at prayer as a relationship with God and not as just making requests. Jesus said that if we abide in him, we will get what we request. A vital part of prayer is worshipping God and expressing praise to him.

The fruit we bear in ministry comes from being connected to Jesus. In Acts 4:13, the people saw the boldness of Peter and John and recognized that they had been with Jesus. When you spend time with Jesus, it will rub off on you. When you read about the ministry of Jesus in the gospels, you see that he was a man of prayer. He was always going off by himself to spend time with his Father. If Jesus needed to pray, then how much more do we need to pray? A minister can only give to others what he receives from God; the place of prayer is where he receives from God.

Psalm 91:1 says, "He who dwells in the secret place of the most high will abide under the shadow of the Almighty." The power of heaven and earth is unlocked when we find a secret place. The first key is finding a secret place, a place where we won't be distracted from fellowshipping with God. God is in the secret place waiting for us to arrive. We also have to find a secret time, a time where we can daily fellowship with God.

Prayer is a two-way conversation. It isn't just talking, but it is listening also. In Matthew 13:9, Jesus said, "He who has ears to hear, let him hear." We don't always have "ears to hear," but they can be developed. Have you ever tried to have a conversation with someone who couldn't hear? It is a one-way conversation and not very much fun. If people can't hear us, we eventually don't want to talk to them. Why waste the effort?

God likes to talk to people who can hear him. In prayer, not only do we make requests, but we take time to hear and meditate. Jesus said that his "sheep hear his voice." It should be natural for us to hear his voice. He is always speaking, but the question is whether we are listening.

God has called the church to prayer, and that is never a fad. No church or ministry will go very far that doesn't have prayer established in it. We are in warfare, and prayer is the foundation. Any ministry endeavor has to be birthed in prayer and born of the Spirit of God. We can adopt all kinds of programs in our church. We can even draw a crowd, but that doesn't mean that we are building a church. If we are doing what God has called us to do, then God is obligated to his Word. God watches over his Word to perform it, and you will see it come to pass.

A pastor needs his private prayer life to be effective, but he also has to teach his church to pray. The best way to teach people to pray is for them to pray with you. Our church has had corporate prayer meetings for years. I've always called prayer a ministry of the church. It is the foundational ministry of the church. Without it, nothing else is as effective as it would be with prayer ministry.

Sadly, many Christians go about the business of their ministry activities without the direction and empowerment that prayer provides. God said that his house would be called a "House of Prayer."

Prayer makes God the center of attention, and the primary purpose of the church is to worship God. I'm not trying to downplay winning souls and making disciples, but if we aren't in right relationship with God, we won't be winning any souls. That is where the church in America is right now.

Prayer is listed as one of the weapons of spiritual warfare in Ephesians chapter 6. In Ephesians 6:18 the apostle Paul said, "Praying with all prayer and supplication in the Spirit." One translation says, "with all types of prayer." So there are many different types of prayer that include worship, intercession, and praying in the Spirit. We are supposed to pray with all of them.

Chapter 5

My Philosophy of Ministry

A successful life is built from the inside out.

—B. B. Hankins

Jesus Christ was the perfect example for ministry. After him, the apostles are the next best example for us.

Our attitude in ministry will determine our success in ministry. When God uses us to help people, they will praise us, but we have to remember that we are just an instrument that God uses to help people. God uses people differently according to their gifts. I want to live my life in such a way that when I am finished, my life will bring glory to God.

Jesus came to seek and save the lost. That was his main purpose. We read in Luke 4:18 that he came to preach the gospel to the poor, heal the brokenhearted, proclaim liberty to the captives, and liberate those who are oppressed.

Philippians chapter 2 says that Jesus humbled himself and became obedient to the cross. God still honors that kind of attitude today. We must have the attitude of a servant. That has to be our philosophy of ministry. Jesus said that those who desire to be first should be servant of all.

When people think of serving, they often think of cleaning the church, mowing the church yard, or cooking a meal. Those are all types of service, but a pastor's primary areas of service are in prayer, study of the Word, teaching the Word, caring for people, and overseeing the church's business.

A pastor's priorities should be his relationship with God first, his caring for the people second, and church administration third. If I don't have a strong personal relationship with God, then I will fail, and the other two won't matter. As a pastor I am willing to do anything that needs to be done. However, I also know that in a larger church that I must delegate for the church to operate efficiently. I can't physically do everything, and even if I could, the church would not operate as efficiently as it could if I involve other people.

We hire a staff to handle the church administration and business, and we train church members to do the work of the ministry. It would be foolish for me to try to do everything when there are people who don't have the leadership responsibilities that I do who are eager for an opportunity to serve and minister. Others will not develop their ministry gifts unless I give them an opportunity to minister.

According to Ephesians 4:11–12, Christ gave the ministry of pastor to perfect the saints for the work of the ministry so that they would build up the church. My job is to train the saints so that they can do the work of the ministry. What is the work of the ministry? The work of the ministry centers around the Great Commission that Jesus gave the church. The book of Matthew says we are to "teach all nations and baptize them." Mark says to go into all the world and preach the gospel. Ministry is both evangelism and discipleship, but I would add the ministries of prayer, serving, and caring for others to those two primary activities that are commanded in the Great Commission. Every Christian should be involved in those five ministries. I serve as the leader, vision caster, teacher, and decision maker and I train and delegate the work of the ministry to those under me.

I would never have been satisfied to be a private chaplain to a handful of Christians. I had to see beyond the four walls of the church. The apostle Paul said that he knew how to be abased and how to abound. That was a classic statement. Paul's level of success did not affect his attitude toward ministry. He knew who he was and what his gift and calling in Christ were.

We need to take time to read Paul's instructions to Timothy. The apostle Paul said, "We labor." You can't be lazy and be in ministry. Those who think they are looking for an easy life in the ministry will never be successful. You have to give everything to it. You can't be a clock-watcher and be in ministry.

The apostle Paul said, "This one thing I do." We must keep the purposes of God in our life. One mistake that ministers make is comparing themselves to one another. If we do that, then we are foolish. We are supposed to do what God has called us to do. I like to go to conferences and see what other people are doing, but I know that I would be foolish to compare myself to them.

I've had opportunities to go off in other directions. When I first started, I sold family Bibles and painted houses to pay the bills. That was only temporary until I could devote all my time to ministry. I've seen many ministers pursue business interests and leave their purpose. In the end we will have to answer to God for the talents that he has put in our hands. God's reward will be worth more than money.

In 1958 I had a minister friend come and visit me. He had a brand-new car, and I was driving an old used car. I have to admit that I was a little envious. God reminded me that I was investing my money in my four children, whose lives would affect eternity.

You will sometimes see situations that you consider to be an inequity, but that is when you have to remember your calling. I would like to be able to say, with the apostle Paul, "I have finished my course." All God requires of you and me is to serve our generation in the will of God.

Chapter 6
MAINTAINING SUCCESSFUL MARRIAGE AND FAMILY RELATIONSHIPS IN MINISTRY

Rules without relationship lead to rebellion.

—B. B. Hankins

A minister's first ministry is to his family. You have to minister to your family before you can minister to others.

First Timothy 3:5 tells us that if a man can't rule his own house, how can he rule the house of God? A church is a spiritual family, and a pastor is a spiritual father. If you can't father your own family, then how can you father a larger family? In many cases when a minister loses his family through divorce, he loses his ministry. That means that your marriage and family must be your top priority.

A good father has a heart of love for his children. A father can't be selfish and be an effective father. In the same way, a spiritual father has to have a heart of love for his spiritual children. Our heavenly Father is the best example of a father that we can have. Jesus revealed to us what the Father is like when he told the parable of the prodigal son. The father in that parable was loving, merciful, and forgiving. That is what our heavenly Father is.

Our wife has to be involved in ministry with us because we are supposed to be one together. Our role as a husband is a redemptive position. Ephesians 5:25 says, "Husbands, love your wives as Christ also loved the church and gave himself for her." We have a greater impact on our wives than anyone else does. We have to stand for them, protect them, and help them fulfill their calling. There cannot be any selfishness on our part because the Word says to put them first. Colossians 3:19 says, "Husbands, love your wives and do not be bitter toward them." The Lord called my attention to that verse many years ago.

Women are more sensitive than we are and we can often say things that offend them. God told me that Velma was not only my wife, but she was a member of the body of Christ. How I treat her is how I treat Jesus. The Holy Spirit can really correct us in that area. Our wives are partners in our lives and partners in ministry, and we can't flow in the anointing if we aren't in right relationship with them. I've found out by experience that one of the greatest needs in ministers' wives is for them to know their place and value by their husband's side. The husband is the one who has to establish that, because your estimation of your wife is very important to her. We also have to establish our wife's value in the church as our partner by our side. The church will follow the minister's estimation of his wife. Some people want to treat your wife as a second-class citizen, but whatever I am is what she is. The Holy Spirit will bring you together where you have the same vision for ministry.

Our wife is also our protector in addition to being our partner. Praising her in public will keep other women from being interested in you. We need to be best friends with our wives, and we need to enjoy each other's company. If we aren't meeting her needs for conversation and communication, then she will talk to someone else. Your wife doesn't need to talk to someone else in the church about her personal problems. We have to take time to communicate together. I've found that my wife sometimes wants to talk about things that I'm not interested in. I know that I have to discipline myself to listen because it is important to her. It is amazing some of the things that women see that we don't even notice.

There has to be the right balance of family and ministry. I also know that if you neglect your ministry, you will be without a job, and you'll have plenty of family time. Some ministers spend time on unimportant things when they could be at home. Sometimes the wife ends up blaming the ministry when in actuality the husband wasn't spending his time on ministry but on other things.

We must also make time for our children while we have the opportunity. There is nothing in life more valuable than our children, and the years that we have with them are short. Our children shouldn't have to grow up resenting the ministry.

Some people are not thoughtful about your time and I've found that many problems can wait until another time. Most problems don't just show up. They took years to develop, and if so, then they can wait one more day. You need to set an appointment to meet with people later when you have planned a family activity. We also have to be careful about discussing church problems in front of our children. That can cause them to be bitter toward ministry. My children thought that everyone in our church was perfect because we never discussed people's faults in front of our children. When you come home at night, leave your problems at the church, or your whole life will be dominated by problems.

We have to learn to love our wives sexually as we love ourselves. It is important to understand her needs, and sometimes that can take a process of years. I've told men before that sex doesn't begin in the bedroom; it begins in the kitchen or living room. Women can't be turned on sexually as quickly as a man. The sexual relationship is determined by how we treat them all day long. Our attitude either turns a woman on or it turns her off.

Some husbands only show their wives attention when they want sex. If you have a frigid wife, it is because you haven't learned how to warm her up. Some women have been through painful experiences, and it takes a lot of patience on the husband's part to meet their needs. Sex for a woman begins with communication and conversation. Emotional intimacy needs to precede physical intimacy. A woman needs affirmation and to know that you think highly of her. Affirmation will boost your sexual relationship, and criticism will decimate it. Women need to hear how beautiful they are and how much you enjoy having sex with them. Women also need nonsexual touching. They need a physical expression of love with no strings attached.

When a husband fulfills his wife's emotional needs, it helps her relax and refuel. A wife also needs time for sexual arousal and foreplay before sexual intercourse. In fact, the arousal period before intercourse can be the most enjoyable part of the sexual experience.

Husbands have a need for intimacy also, and their need is fulfilled more by sexual expression than by conversation or nonsexual touching. Sexual expression allows men to remove the walls that keep them from intimacy with their wives. A husband's self-esteem is related to his sexual performance, and it is important to him that his wife is a willing sex partner. When a wife wants to have sex with her husband, he is thrilled because it means that his wife finds him desirable. The husband wants the wife to take an interest in the activity that he enjoys the most. When a wife says no, in his mind, she is rejecting not just sex but him. Husbands also have to be sensitive to knowing the right time to initiate sexual relations. When the wife is tired and under pressure, she won't respond positively to his advances.

As ministers we also have to be very careful about counseling women. I won't discuss a woman's sex life with her, and I always refer those types of discussions to my wife. I know of many ministers who have fallen into a snare by counseling with women. When a beautiful woman wants our advice, it strokes our ego. I know that some women think it would be wonderful to be married to a minister, but if they just talked to your wife, they would find out different. When they see us in church, they don't know about all of our faults. I let women counsel women and I won't counsel a woman unless my wife is with me. This policy also protects me from people's suspicions and false accusations that could arise.

The sexual relationship between husband and wife is important. That is why the apostle Paul said in 1 Corinthians 7:5, "Do not deprive one another except with consent for a time." The reason that Paul gave was so that Satan would not be able to tempt either partner with sex outside their marriage relationship. When the sexual relationship in a marriage is good, there is no need to look elsewhere to get your needs met. Many wives need to understand this. The sexual relationship brings a bonding and intimacy between husband and wife that nothing else can bring. God created sex so that a man and woman could give physical expression to the love they have for each other emotionally. That makes it important. God wants our marriage to be a means of happiness and fulfillment in all areas of our life together.

The sexual relationship is the barometer of the marriage relationship. It gauges how well the entire relationship is functioning. When the relationship is going well, the result will be intimacy between the husband and wife. When other areas of the relationship aren't up to par, it will be reflected in the sexual relationship. Strife in the home will kill the desire for a sexual relationship.

Men consider sex to be intimacy, and women consider talking to be intimacy. Satisfying sex occurs when the husband and wife connect the physical with the emotional. That is why the way we treat our mate will determine whether they want to be intimate with us. No one wants to be intimate with someone they are angry with. Both husband and wife must treat each other with kindness to create an atmosphere for sexual intimacy. That means controlling our tongue when our partner or life's circumstances irritate us.

To get our needs met in marriage, we have to meet our mate's needs. Meeting your mate's needs begins with the right attitude of wanting to meet their needs. The second step is communication with your mate about what they desire in the sexual experience. You can't just give your mate what satisfies you, but ask what satisfies them.

Communication between husband and wife will help provide a satisfying experience for both. God created us as sexual beings because a sexual relationship is an important part of marriage. There was no such thing as "sex" before God created it. Sex was God's idea. In the marriage relationship sex is pure and undefiled and pleasing to God.

When there is harmony in the home, there is harmony in your

ministry. The hardest conditions to minister in are when there is strife in your marriage or family. That is why the apostle Paul said to make every effort to keep the unity of the Spirit. He was writing to the church at Ephesus, but it certainly applies to our families also.

Many ministers are successful at ministry, but they fail as a husband and father. It is a tragedy to see someone win the world but lose their own children. If you make your family your priority, it won't happen to you.

Chapter 7

THE ANOINTING OF THE HOLY SPIRIT

Spiritual battles are not won by the hand of the flesh.

—B. B. Hankins

You and I know that the most precious gift for ministry is the anointing of the Holy Spirit. There is not anything worse than trying to preach without him. I am like Moses in that if the Lord is not going with me, then I don't want to go.

I like to read Jesus's sermon in Luke 4:18. He was in the synagogue in Nazareth where he grew up, and as his custom was, he went into the synagogue. I like that. Jesus had a habit of going to church. He took the book of Isaiah and read from chapter 61: "The spirit of the Lord is upon me because he has anointed me to preach the Gospel to the poor, he has sent me to heal the broken hearted, preach liberty to the captives, and the recovering of sight to the blind."

Jesus only had to say once that he was anointed, because the fruit of the anointing was evident in his life. You know a preacher is in trouble when he has to keep repeating that the anointing is upon him. Some preachers have to keep saying, "God is in this place," but the people will know if God is there.

There is no sense in talking about the anointing to someone who doesn't know what it is. My simple definition of the anointing is this: The anointing is a substance that will allow you to do what you can't do in the natural. Jesus said in Luke 4 that he was anointed to preach the gospel to the poor, to proclaim liberty to the captives, and proclaim the acceptable year of the Lord. Jesus said that he was anointed to do six things, and three of them were preaching.

I've always believed that no matter what you have in a church service, you should always have preaching. I've been criticized for that, and people have even left my church over that issue. They thought that I was trying to quench the revival. I believe that preaching the Word is a priority.

If people want to go to a church where all they do is jump and holler with no preaching, let them go somewhere else. I believe in jumping and hollering, or I could not have lived with my wife and had peace. It took Velma and the Holy Spirit forty-nine years to get me to dance in church. One preacher said that the next best thing to going to heaven is to preach under the anointing of the Holy Spirit. When the presence of God comes upon you, it will turn you into another man.

I've had times while pastoring churches when I didn't have good worship leaders. I even used to lead worship myself and then preach. I could be in a service that was dead as a hammer, and if I allowed myself to be anointed, the glory of God would fall into that church. I learned to depend on God so that before I got through preaching, the anointing of God would be in that place. There were a few services when I wanted to slip out the back door because there was no power. When the service was a disappointment, I always knew that I was going to show up next week and preach again. We need mighty preaching of the Word of God. Preach the Word.

In the days of the charismatic revival I was involved with the Full Gospel Business Men's Fellowship. I had a friend named F. E. Ward who was a real prophet of God. He had a great influence on our family and our church. He was involved in the Full Gospel Business Men's Fellowship and also ministered to many denominational pastors and led them into the baptism of the Holy Spirit.

In those days when a denominational preacher would get the baptism of the Holy Spirit, he would get kicked out of his church, and he wouldn't have anywhere to minister. These preachers would go all around the country and give their testimony. The problem is that if all you have is a testimony to give, you can only preach at a church one time.

I had another friend by the name of Arthur Locke. He was homeless on the streets of Houston when he got saved. They called him the Mayor of Capital Avenue because he used to be an oilman before he became homeless, and his friends in the oil business would give him their old suits. He was the best-dressed bum on the streets. Arthur Locke had been arrested over two hundred times. He came to West Columbia after he was saved and gave his testimony, which was one of the best testimonies that I have ever heard. The next time he came back and preached a three-night revival. Then finally he came and preached a seven-day revival which was the longest that he had ever preached in one place before. His ministry really took off when he learned to preach under the anointing of the Holy Spirit.

It is important for a minister to know how to preach. It takes some effort to study the Word and have something to say, but I believe that it is worth the effort. If God has called you to preach, then prepare yourself to be able to proclaim the truth of God's Word.

Chapter 8

Integrity in Ministry

Everything you gain by compromise, you will eventually lose.

—B. B. Hankins

One of the greatest needs in the ministry and in the body of Christ today is integrity. You have probably thought at times that you were in covenant relationship with people, but they just walked off as if the relationship never meant anything to them. Some people leave a church and never even say good-bye or why they are leaving. That is not even good manners, much less integrity.

The dictionary says that integrity is a firm adherence to a code of moral values. The word *integrity* comes from a root that means "whole." It implies that there is congruence between what I say and what I do.

To have integrity is to be followers and practitioners of our own deep spiritual and moral values. We have to learn to submit our feelings, impulses, and moods to the spiritual and moral values we possess. The famous playwright Arthur Miller said that integrity was bigger than telling the truth; it was being a certain kind of person.

Having integrity is being people who know who we are and what we are. It is being true to what we are, even when it would cost us more than we want to pay. We need the kind of integrity that perseveres in persecution, resists temptation, obeys God's Word, overcomes prejudice, produces good works, controls the tongue, follows God's wisdom, and considers how our actions affect others.

What do our actions say to other people? I like Evangelist Joel Cook because he knows how to behave himself in the churches where he is ministering. Some of our church members were over at his home visiting him, and they began to criticize our church leadership. He told them that if they were going to criticize, then they didn't need to come over to his home anymore.

You can agree with someone and never say a word. All you have to do is keep quiet and listen. There is not a bigger fool in the world than someone who believes only one side of a story. Once a member of my church came and asked me questions about things that other people had said to him. He told them that if they had problems or issues, then they needed to come and talk to me. There is not a bigger pain in the neck than a "wannabe" preacher in your church who causes trouble.

There is not a greater book in the Bible about integrity than the book of James. The book of James says that genuine faith should make a difference in the way people live, what they respect, and whom they respect. Our faith can't be expressed in word only; it has to be expressed in action. James was Jesus's brother and lived with Jesus for thirty years. He believed that Jesus was the Messiah and became the head of the church at Jerusalem.

The first twelve verses in James are the test of integrity. He says that a double-minded man will receive nothing from the Lord. Integrity holds fast to what it believes and trusts God to do what he said he would do. The church was being persecuted when James wrote about the trial of our faith. Persecution to them meant loss of life for their faith. Today we think it is persecution if someone speaks badly about us. Real Christianity is rejoicing in trouble and not just when we feel the anointing. The word *faith* is only mentioned twice in the entire Old Testament, but in the book of James it is mentioned sixteen times.

Conflicts in the church may just be conflicts in our personal life. Integrity in ministry begins with keeping our word. Do what you tell others you are going to do. If you raise money for a project, then spend the money on that project. Keep your word to others in your ministry and business dealings. Make sure that your church or ministry pays its bills. Nothing will give your church or ministry a worse reputation than not paying your bills. Our church has always presented an annual financial statement to our members so they can see how much came in and how it was spent.

Integrity in pastoral ministry means not trying to steal another pastor's sheep by manipulation or intentionally trying to develop a relationship with people who are members of another church for the sole purpose of getting them to join your church. Integrity is not bad-mouthing other churches or pastors to induce people to leave their church and come to yours. We see integrity when staff pastors are loyal to their senior pastor, and when they leave to take their own church, they don't try to take their senior pastor's church members with them.

Anyone who would want a gossip or someone who bad-mouths other pastors is not very spiritually discerning. Pastors who do those things usually reap what they sow. The joke is on them because they end up getting all the other church's rebels, and then the rebels turn on them after they have been at their church for a few years. A few years ago a new pastor came to our area and he went after everyone else's sheep. He got a lot of people to hop to his church but eventually they turned against him, and he had to leave. The biggest red flag is when someone new comes to your church and they are criticizing their former church and pastor but telling you how wonderful you are. It won't be long until they leave your church saying the same thing about you.

Integrity for a minister means living what you preach. I've heard preachers joking around after they got through preaching, by saying, "I'm just glad I don't have to live it." You shouldn't be preaching anything that you don't live. A parent can't tell his children to "Do as I say, not as I do." However, your children will do as you do. The same principle applies to spiritual fathers. We have to practice what we preach. I love to hear preachers who have accomplished great things. That makes their preaching mean something. They aren't talking about something that they haven't experienced, but you know that they have lived what they are preaching about.

The best way to develop integrity is to read the Word of God and then put it into practice. When you practice the Word of God, you walk in integrity. The book of Proverbs provides sound instruction on walking in integrity in our relationships with people. It will instruct us on the practical aspects of human relationships.

I've read a chapter a day in the book of Proverbs for years, and I know that it has helped me with human relationships. I want to encourage you to make the book of Proverbs a part of your daily Bible reading. Let's be examples to the world and be people whose words and actions match.

Chapter 9

How to Prepare Sermons

Jesus never commissioned anyone to preach a gospel
that didn't include healing the sick.

—B. B. Hankins

One of the biggest challenges in pastoral ministry is the pulpit ministry. An evangelist can preach the same sermons at different churches or conferences, but a pastor has to have new sermons every week. I have had to preach three sermons a week for years, so I know what it means to be instant in season.

You can preach out of your heart, but if you aren't careful, you will preach the same things over and over. Preaching out of your heart is great if you are constantly putting new truths into your heart. I know that truth has to be restated, but leftovers get old after the second time.

The hardest part of preaching a sermon is finding a sermon. Finding a subject or key text is half of writing a sermon. The best way to find new messages is to let them develop out of your private prayer and Bible study. If you have a daily time of feeding yourself on the Word of God, you will have new messages As you read the Word of God, passages will stand out and minister to you. From those Scriptures that God impresses on your heart, you have the first step in writing a message. When you have clear direction, then writing a message is much easier.

Many messages come to me in my prayer time. While I am praying or worshipping, the Holy Spirit will bring a Scripture or phrase to my mind. I can feel that this Scripture or word has an anointing with it, and I know that God wants me to proclaim the word he gave me. I've always made my messages a matter of prayer and asked God for the right message. I am led of the Spirit on what to preach.

It is a great joy to preach a message and then have people tell you that the message applied exactly to certain issues that they were dealing with in their life. Your pulpit ministry is a reflection of your personal relationship with God. If you aren't hearing from God, then the people you minister to won't hear from God either.

It's wonderful when the Holy Spirit gives me clear-cut direction with a Scripture or a message to preach. Unfortunately, that is not always the case. When I don't have clear-cut direction, then I have to study and search for the right message. The apostle Paul told Timothy to study so that he could be "approved by God." That means that you will have to study the Word of God to be effective in your preaching ministry. I've found that when I begin to seek a message, then I will find it. While I am seeking for the right message, then the Holy Spirit will give me inspiration to develop that message. I've had times when I've had such inspiration from the Holy Spirit that writing the sermon came quickly and easily. However, most of the time it is hard work.

A preacher's most important ministry is to God in prayer and worship. A pastor is the primary intercessor for his church because he is most aware of the problems that need prayer. One of the ways that we shepherd our flock is by praying for our sheep. After prayer his second most important responsibility is his preaching ministry. His third most important responsibility is caring for his congregation.

Administration falls fourth on the list of priorities. We hire a staff to handle the administrative duties of the church so we can focus on our most important priorities. Administrative tasks are necessary in ministry, but a minister who neglects prayer and preaching to spend most of his time on administrative tasks will eventually fail in ministry. I'm not saying that a pastor doesn't oversee his staff and make the important decisions, because he has to do that. A pastor shouldn't handle the church offerings, but he should oversee them and manage the finances. I've seen small churches hire a pastor because he was a good handyman who could do the church maintenance. The first qualification for a pastor is to be a man of prayer and the Word who can feed the sheep. Find a church member who is a good handyman to do maintenance, or hire someone else to do those tasks.

A pastor has to preach to address the spiritual needs of his congregation. Most often those needs become obvious over time. For instance, if the congregation is not tithing and giving, you know what you need to preach on. If they aren't faithful in church attendance, you need to preach on the importance of assembling together for worship and hearing the Word. If you know that there is strife and backbiting in the church, then you need to preach on biblical conflict resolution and controlling the tongue. If no one is winning souls, you need to preach on how to become a soul winner.

Our job is to equip our people, so that they can do the work of the ministry. I preach on the subject of prayer regularly. The ministry of the Holy Spirit is one of my favorite topics. I love to preach on the person of Jesus, not only his ministry on the earth but also his death and resurrection.

The key to being a good preacher is spending time feeding yourself spiritually. I not only read the Word, but I also listen to what other men and women of God have to say. I buy books and tapes so I can hear the Word preached while I am driving and also at home. I attend conferences and revivals so I can be ministered to and refreshed.

When my church was small and times were challenging, I would go to the Full Gospel Business Men's meetings in Houston on Saturdays so I could be ministered to. If I hadn't gotten the encouragement I needed in those meetings, I don't know if I would have made it in ministry. I went to Tulsa several times to minister's conferences hosted by Dr. Kenneth E. Hagin and Oral Roberts. I always left feeling encouraged and strengthened. Faith comes by hearing and hearing again. When you stop hearing the Word, your faith level will drop. If anyone in the church needs strong faith, it is the pastor.

Finally, the best messages come out of your life experiences. When you have experienced the faithfulness and grace of God in your life, you can preach it as no one else could. I am so moved by the testimonies of people who were saved out of a life of sin. They still cry when they are telling their testimony, even if it is thirty years later. They can tell their story from their heart. In the same way, look back on the challenges that God has brought you through, and tell about his faithfulness.

I've always been amazed at how well God takes care of me for fulfilling the responsibilities of preaching his Word. I believe the call to preach is the greatest vocation in the world. You have the chance to change the eternal destiny of the people you preach to, and that should never be taken lightly.

Chapter 10

THE CHURCH THAT OVERCOMES

A lack of prayer is a lack of humility.

—B. B. Hankins

Jesus said to the church at Philadelphia in Revelation 3:8, "I have set before thee an open door, and no man can shut it." So the church in Philadelphia was the church of the open door.

I believe that the book of Revelation was addressed to real, local churches. Most theologians apply the open door to missions and outreach. Historians say that for one thousand years the Philadelphia church led the churches of Asia in missionary outreach. A thousand years is a sustained movement. Some churches can't last for ten years.

John goes on in Revelation 4:1 to talk about a door that was opened for him to enter into the throne room of heaven. John found himself in the control room of God's eternal purposes. He sees God on the throne and the twenty-four elders around the throne. These twenty-four elders represent the church both in heaven and on earth. Part of the church is in heaven and part of the church is on the earth. In other words, believers don't die, they just change locations. I have said many times that I join with the prayers of my parents in heaven for my family members who are still here on the earth.

The Philadelphia church enters into that door in heaven to share in intercession before the throne. The Philadelphia church goes through the door that no man can shut and positions herself with

Christ in the heavenlies. From her place with Christ the church joins together with Christ in intercession. This type of intercessory ministry will effectively release upon the earth spiritual forces that will bring harvest to the earth.

The Open Door Church releases the will of God on the earth as it is in heaven. I've been to meetings where the glory of God swept into the church in a mighty way, and people were moved to seek God. Anytime you see that, you can be sure that there were people behind the scenes whose intercession in the heavenlies caused the power of God to be released on earth. All victories that take place in public are won in private. Spiritual victories are won in the throne room before they are manifested down here. Hebrew 10:19 says that we "have boldness to enter into the holy of holies by the blood of Jesus, which is our new and living way." The blood of Jesus is our doorway into heaven.

What an honor we have to be invited into the throne room of God. We have an invitation to intercede with the church in heaven. Jesus taught us to pray that God's will may be done on earth as it is in heaven. Prayer is not begging God to do something or overcoming his reluctance to do something. Prayer is enforcing Christ's victory over Satan and the world. The enforcement of Calvary's victory was placed in our hands. We are destined to reign with Christ, and God has chosen us to be partners to fulfill his plan on the earth.

In Matthew 18:18 Jesus said, "Whatsoever you shall bind on earth will be bound in heaven, and whatsoever you shall loose on earth will be loosed in heaven." Authority has been delegated to the church to enforce the will of God upon the earth. Jesus told the church that all authority was given to him in heaven and earth, so we are to go in his name.

We bind and loose in two ways. The first way is by speaking the Word of God, and the second way is by prayer. We stand around and ask ourselves, "Why doesn't God do something?" while God is looking down from heaven wondering, "Why doesn't the church do something?" E. M. Bounds said, "Prayer is striking the winning blow, service is gathering the results." Prayer is the primary business of the church. A prayerless church is a powerless church.

In Ezekiel chapter 22, God wants to spare the nation of Israel and avoid judging the nation. God looked for a man who could intercede for the nation and he could not find one, so he poured out his wrath upon Israel. That speaks volumes to us about interceding for our nation. It means that God needs us to be involved.

Jack Hayford said, "Prayer is a partnership consisting of us and God working toward the fulfillment of God's purposes in the earth." We are colaborers together with God. Jesus was our intercessor on the cross, and he is still our intercessor in heaven. We too have been given a ministry of reconciliation and intercession. Intercession is bringing people into contact with God. Our prayers and intercession are an extension of Jesus's work of intercession. Intercession is Jesus interceding through us.

One of the laws of prayer is the law of faith. We must believe that we have received before we do receive. Not everything is up to God. Individual responsibility and free will also determine what happens on the earth. Some Christians are offended if you suggest that unbelief kept them from receiving. Yet the book of James says that a "double-minded man will receive nothing from God." The Bible also says that if we won't forgive, then God will not answer our prayers. God is the performer, and we are the believer. Abraham believed that God was able to perform what he had promised. Abraham waited for twenty-five years but he was strong in faith and gave glory to God. You can tell if people are strong in faith by whether they are praising or worrying and complaining.

One of the greatest keys to intercession is to cooperate with the Holy Spirit. The Holy Spirit is our helper, and one of the areas that he helps us is in our prayer life. Romans 8:26 says that we don't always know what to pray for and how to pray for situations, but the Holy Spirit makes intercession for us with groanings that cannot be uttered. I believe that this Scripture refers to interceding in other tongues or interceding in the Spirit. The Holy Spirit can help us pray as we pray "in the Spirit." The Holy Spirit will cause our prayers to touch the right person and bring forth the will of God. The Holy Spirit takes hold with us and adds his strength to ours. When the Holy Spirit takes hold with us, then things have to move.

It doesn't take me a long time to pray with the natural knowledge that I have about a situation. That is when I move into another dimension of prayer, which is praying in the spirit. What a great privilege we have to enter before the throne of God and obtain help from him. When we intercede, we don't intercede alone. We have the host of heaven joining with us. Let's walk through the door that God has given us.

Chapter 11

THE SECRET TO OVERCOMING
HARD SITUATIONS

You can't fail if you don't quit.

—B. B. Hankins

I've heard ministers call cities and churches "preachers' graveyards," and I've heard missionaries call countries "missionaries' graveyards." I've heard pastors say, "This is a hard church to pastor." I've got news for them: they are all hard to pastor.

I once asked a fellow pastor how his church was doing, and he said, "This one is going down slower than the last one." He was a church "planter": he planted them all in the ground.

When I first came to West Columbia, it was difficult to preach the Word here. I had just been here a few months when my father came down to preach a revival for me. He didn't say anything negative when he was here, but after he left and went home, he told my mother that West Columbia was the hardest place he had ever preached in his life. My mother told me what he had said, and I was relieved because I knew then that it wasn't just me. Oppression, sickness, and financial problems were coming against me. I found my answers to overcoming hard situations from the Word of God and the Holy Spirit's personal revelation to me.

In Matthew chapter 17 a man brought his demon-possessed son

to Jesus's disciples for them to cure him. Jesus's disciples couldn't cure his son, so he brought him to Jesus. Jesus rebuked his disciples' lack of faith, and then he cast the evil spirit out of the boy. Jesus's disciples later asked him why they couldn't cast the evil spirit out, but he could. Jesus gave them three answers, and these are the three keys to overcoming hard situations.

The first reason that Jesus gave his disciples as to why they couldn't cast the demon out was their unbelief. When I was struggling with the hard situations after moving to West Columbia, a missionary from Mexico came to speak at our church. He preached on faith that was contrary to what we discern with our five senses. I'd had faith taught to me all my life, but not like that. I was desperate physically, spiritually, financially, and emotionally. That missionary spoke for an hour and a half about how to walk by faith and not by sight. I wouldn't have cared if he had preached all night because my wife was at home sick in bed, I had two small children, and I couldn't pay my bills. I began to read books on faith, and I got a grasp on the fact that the devil is a defeated foe and the authority that we have in Christ. I began to take authority over the oppression and lack and stand in faith on the promises of God. That was my first key to overcoming in a hard situation.

In Matthew 17:21, Jesus gives his disciples the other two keys to overcoming hard situations. He tells them, "This kind does not go out except by prayer and fasting." The tough devils are cast out by prayer and fasting. It is obvious from what Jesus said that his disciples were not practicing prayer and fasting. When Jesus was struggling in prayer in the garden of Gethsemane, his disciples couldn't even pray with him for an hour. The disciples' lack of prayer was one of the reasons for their lack of power.

Prayer is fellowship and communication with God. It is much more than just asking for something. Prayer is relationship with God. Praise and worship are a vital part of prayer and are also the proper protocol for approaching God. When Jesus told his disciples that lack of prayer was the reason they couldn't cast out the evil spirit, he wasn't just talking about the prayer of petition. He was talking about a lifestyle of worship and communication with God. Making petitions is certainly part of prayer, but it is not the only part. There is also listening to what God says to us. To hear God's voice, I have to slow down and get into his presence. Jesus called this worship "in spirit and in truth." You don't learn the mind of God with a daily five-minute prayer time. God said he would direct our paths if we would acknowledge him in all our ways. Jesus had the power to cast the evil spirit out because he lived a lifestyle of fellowship with the Father.

Jesus didn't say that prayer alone was one of the keys to overcoming, but he said, "Prayer and fasting." I believe that fasting is more than just doing without food. Fasting means denying yourself. Jesus said that if any man was going to follow him, he must deny himself. That means denying our own selfish desires to do the will of God. The fruits of the Holy Spirit in us are the result of living a fasted life. The Word says that if we walk in the Spirit, we won't fulfill the desires of the flesh.

Fasting is also controlling your thoughts and your words. Some people need to fast leisure and recreation so they can do the will of God. Everyone needs recreation and relaxation, but if it keeps us from prayer and serving in a local church, then it is out of control. Fasting is separating ourselves from the natural activities and distractions and connecting with God. We don't fast to try and get God to act in our behalf, because we are justified by faith.

I wrestled with this Scripture for years until one day the Holy Spirit spoke to me and said, "You'll never have authority over demons until you have authority over yourself. You won't cast out the hard kind until you have authority over yourself. You won't overcome hard situations until you have authority over yourself."

The Holy Spirit began to deal with me about fasting. It's one thing to know who you are in Christ, and it's another thing to bring your flesh under the authority of the Holy Spirit. When you see a fruitful life or a fruitful ministry, there is something behind it. There is someone who has denied his or her own self to do God's will and bring forth a bountiful harvest.

I began to fast, but I didn't tell everyone what I was doing. I first fasted for seven days, then for fourteen days, and then for twenty-one days. I didn't feel a great anointing or great power when I did it, but it did something for my inner man and my will. I used to weigh 265 pounds years ago. I didn't have a problem going on a diet because I had been on hundreds of them. I especially didn't have a problem going on any diet that would start tomorrow. I broke a weakness in me that I had not been able to master in all my life.

After that the Lord led me to live a fasted life. I never had to go on another twenty-one-day fast. The end of the story is that I came out of the hard situation. My wife got well, the church grew, and I'm not poor anymore. I saw the hard things conquered, and you can too.

Chapter 12

How to Get More of What You Need

Whatever you need, sow that kind of seed.

—B. B. Hankins

In Matthew 25:29, Jesus said, "For unto everyone that hath shall be given, and he shall have abundance: but from him that hath not shall be taken away even that which he hath." This is a law of God. To everyone that has, more shall be given.

That is shocking, isn't it? God says that if we are willing to put to use what he has already given us, we will have more. If we are not willing to use what God has given us, we will lose it. Jesus did not intend to give us a principle to make the rich get richer and the poor get poorer. He was showing us how the "Law of Use" works.

If we exercise the gifts that God has already given us, we will gain more gifts and more provision. If you take what you have and use it, it will increase. A few weeks ago I started doing some push-ups to get my body in better shape. I did three push-ups, and it was hard on me. I continued to do push-ups every week, and now I am up to sixteen push-ups. I know that sixteen push-ups is nothing to people who can do a hundred push-ups. How did I go from three to sixteen push-ups? By the "Law of Use." If you use what you have, it will increase. Initially it was hard for me to do three push-ups because for several years I didn't exercise, and I was losing what I was not using.

Jesus tells the parable of the talents beginning in Matthew 25:14.

A master who is going on a journey gives his goods to his servants to use them while he is gone. This master gives to one servant five talents, another servant two talents, and the last servant one talent.

The servant who has received five talents invests the master's money and doubles it. The servant who received two talents invests the master's money and doubles his portion. The servant who received one talent, however, digs a hole in the ground and hides the master's money. The master of the servants returns home and demands an accounting of the talents that he has given his servants.

The servants who received five talents and the two talents both tell the master that they have doubled his talents. The master tells each of them, "Well done, my good and faithful servant: thou hast been faithful over a few things, I will make thee ruler over many things." However, the servant who received one talent tells his master that he was afraid of him and hid his talent. The master is angry and takes the talent from him to give it to the servant who now has ten talents.

The master in this parable represents God, and we are the servants. One day we will all stand before God and give an account of our stewardship of the talents that he has given us. God expects us to take whatever talents he has given us and improve them, whether it is preaching, serving, musical gifts, or occupational skills. Proper use of what he had been given gave the man with ten talents even more talents. The man with one talent was punished for improper use. He wasn't going to use what had been given him, and it was taken away from him.

Another story in the Bible that shows how God uses what we have is found in 2 Kings chapter 4. It is the story of a widow who is broke and owes creditors, who are going to come and take her children to repay the debt. She tells the prophet Elisha about her impossible situation, and Elisha asks her what she has in her house. The widow says that she has nothing but a jar of oil.

Elisha tells her to go and borrow all the empty vessels she can from her neighbors and pour the oil she has into them. The widow pours the oil and keeps pouring until all of the vessels are full. She then sells the oil and pays her debt.

You can get your eyes on what you need and not realize that God wants you to use what you already have. When you use what God has already given you, then it will multiply. Often Christians say that they would tithe and give offerings if they had more money. It doesn't work that way. You have to be faithful to tithe and give offerings with what you already have, or God won't give you more.

The Bible says that if we are faithful with a little, then we will be faithful with more. We prove to God that we will be responsible with more if we are responsible with what we have. The same principle applies to our talents and abilities. They never develop until we use them. You'll never be a great preacher until you start preaching. You'll never be a great pastor until you pastor a church. Your gifts don't develop if they are hidden in the ground. You'll never be a spiritual leader until you can be a follower. I've seen people who couldn't even be faithful to attend church think that they were going to lead a church. God doesn't work that way.

The longest journey begins with the first step. God has already given you a seed to sow to bring your harvest in. This widow's jar of oil was just a small, insignificant thing compared to her need. She had overlooked what she already had, and the prophet Elisha had to make her aware of it. Notice that the widow had to take action to receive her miracle. To get what you need you have to exercise faith in God to use what you already have. It also takes faithfulness to keep on believing and acting until the answer comes. If you look at great ministries you will see that none of them started where they are today. All of them started small and were faithful to use what they already had. Use what God has already given you, and he will give you the things that you need.

Chapter 13
THE FATHER'S BUSINESS

Dreamers do a lot of talking, but people of vision do
a lot of doing.

—B. B. Hankins

In Luke chapter 2 there is the story of Joseph's and Mary's trip to Jerusalem with young Jesus for the Feast of Passover. Later they left Jerusalem, thinking that Jesus was with them, but he had stayed behind in Jerusalem. They went back and found him at the temple courts listening to the teachers and asking questions. Jesus was only twelve years old, and the teachers were amazed at the wisdom he had at that age. When Joseph and Mary asked Jesus why he had stayed behind and not left with them, Jesus said that he had to be about his Father's business. Later in his life there was a time when Jesus's disciples came to him and asked him if he had any meat to eat. Jesus told them that his meat was to do the will of "him that sent me" and to finish his work.

Jesus's delight was to do the work of his Father. You work when you do things that you don't enjoy. When you enjoy what you are doing, it is not work to you. If we are Jesus's disciples then our joy should be to do the Father's will.

Romans 8:28 says, "All things work together for good to them who are called according to his purpose." When you are committed to God's plan, then things will work for you every time.

Many people wonder what the will of God for them is. The will of God for you, first of all, is for you to believe the gospel. All things are possible for those who believe. There are people who need Jesus, and we have the answer. The gospel has made provision for every need, whatever it is. Jesus finished his work and sat down at the right hand of the Father, and our place is to ask for God's will to be done on earth.

We have enemies who try to stop us, but we can prevail in prayer. Many things that seem to be the sovereign will of God are the result of people's prayers. They may be prayers that were prayed years ago by people who have already passed on. Jesus said that we have been given authority over all the power of the enemy. We have been raised together and seated together in heavenly places in Christ.

The only thing that you can take to heaven with you is someone else. You can take people you have shared the gospel with who have accepted Jesus. The rich people in heaven will be those who took others with them.

Sometimes I visit communities where my father pastored, and the people love me for my father's sake. I've had people who heard the gospel from my dad say to me with tears in their eyes that my dad brought them the good news. One man who was a bootlegger told me that he was in a mess until my dad came and told him a way out of the mess. When my father left this earth, he didn't leave me one dime. He left me riches far beyond material riches: an inheritance in the gospel. He taught me to believe and have faith in God, and that is all I need. No matter what you face today, if you have faith in God, then nothing is impossible. Our faith is the most important thing that we can leave to our children.

Abraham was a father who was willing to give his only son to God. He taught Isaac to put God first. He was a man of faith who believed that God would fulfill a promise that was impossible to fulfill in the natural. God said of Abraham that he knew that he would command his children to follow in his steps and keep the way of God. What a great honor it is for God to say that about a man.

Abraham's nephew Lot chose money over godliness and it cost him his family. Even Lot's life was saved by Abraham's intercession.

We have a choice in how we lead our family. We begin by committing our own life to the will of God. Will you commit your life to God's purpose for it today?

Chapter 14

WHEN THE HOLY SPIRIT HAS COME

God said it, I believe it, and that settles it.

—B. B. Hankins

Before Jesus ascended into heaven, he told his disciples that they would receive power when the Holy Spirit had come upon them. Jesus was talking about the experience that would begin for them on the day of Pentecost in the upper room. That was the initial outpouring of the Holy Spirit on the early church.

Jesus had previously taught his disciples other truths of how the Holy Spirit would function in their lives. John 14:16 says, "I will pray the Father and He shall give you another Comforter that He may abide with you forever." One of the Holy Spirit's functions is that of a Comforter. The Holy Spirit is able to heal the hurt that we experience in our lives.

In June 1955 my family went to stay at my father's home in Corsicana to attend the wedding of my youngest sister, Jean. My father, Robert Hankins, was a pastor and a presbyter for the Assemblies of God. In the middle of the night my father had a heart attack and died. I will never forget when they took his body out of the house. We were all in a state of shock. We prayed with my mother for a long time that night, and then we went to bed.

As I lay in bed, I experienced the comfort of the Holy Spirit. I felt the everlasting peace of God surrounding me in waves of tenderness, and I felt the gentleness of the Holy Spirit like the comfort of a mother. The next morning when I got up I felt the strength of the Holy Spirit. I had to have strength to handle the funeral arrangements and the family business that followed my father's death. I was facing something that I had never faced before in my life at the age of twenty-six years. The strength of the Holy Spirit enabled me to be strong.

The Greek word that is translated "Comforter" is *paraclete*. It means "one who is called alongside to help." The Holy Spirit is the steel backbone equal to every sorrow, disappointment, and problem that we face. Sometimes when I face a challenging assignment, someone will ask me if I am ready for it. I always say that I will be ready when the time comes. I can say that because the Holy Spirit is my enabler, and he lives in me, so when the time comes I will be ready.

Jesus said in John 14:26, "When the Holy Spirit has come, He will teach us all things." All things means "everything that we have need of." The Holy Spirit not only knows what you need, he knows what God has planned for you, and if you will listen to him, he will teach you.

We haven't been taught until we have learned, and understanding has to come before we can grasp truth. Giving illumination is one of the ministries of the Spirit. One of the things that the Spirit illuminates for us is the Word of God. The Holy Spirit is in agreement with the Word of God, since he helped write it. The Scriptures were given by the inspiration of the Spirit to men. Illumination is not a mystical experience; it is just listening to the Holy Spirit. The Holy Spirit makes us understand God's Word. It is walking in the Spirit as it says in Romans chapter 8. We follow the Holy Spirit's voice instead of the voice of the flesh. The Holy Spirit won't lead us in anything that is not in agreement with God's Word in either doctrine or behavior.

I was invited to teach a Bible study in the home of Ralph Littlejohn in Houston during the 1960s. Ralph was a member of the Evangelistic Temple church in Houston, which was pastored by Austin Wilkerson back then. The first thing I did before I taught in Ralph's home was call Pastor Wilkerson and tell him that a member of his church had invited me to speak in his home. I asked if that was acceptable with him. The Holy Spirit doesn't lead one pastor to do something that would hurt another pastor or his church.

The leading of the Holy Spirit doesn't free us from ethical responsibilities. A man once told me that the Holy Spirit told him to leave his wife. I didn't have to pray about that one because it was in disagreement with the Word of God. Another person told me that the Holy Spirit had said they should give their tithes to their grandmother instead of their local church. Everyone should take care of his or her grandmother if she is in need, but not with their tithe. They should tithe to their church and give an offering above that to their grandmother. The Bible says that the tithe goes to the storehouse, which was the temple in the Old Testament and is the local church today.

In John 16:13, Jesus said that the Holy Spirit will not speak of himself, but he will speak whatever he hears. The Holy Spirit hears what the Father and Jesus are saying and speaks their words to us. In Acts 13:2, the prophets and teachers in the church at Antioch were ministering to the Lord and fasting, and the Holy Spirit said, "Separate me Barnabas and Saul for the work that I have called them to." The Holy Spirit is speaking but we aren't always listening. The Spirit is endeavoring to get our attention. The only security that we have is in hearing the voice of the Spirit and obeying.

He will tell you all you need to know if you will listen to him. First Corinthians 2:12 says, "We have received, not the spirit of the world, but the Spirit which is of God: that we might know the things that are freely given to us of God." Some of the things that are freely given to us by God are a spirit of power, love, and a sound mind.

God wants to deliver you from the spirit of fear. There may come times when fear is an obsession in your life. You don't just fear one thing, but you fear many things. It could be a fear about your health, your finances, your children, or other people. The Holy Spirit has come to make us bold in God so that we aren't afraid of anything. You have the Spirit of power, love, and a well-balanced mind.

Chapter 15

FAITH, THE HOLY SPIRIT, AND MIRACLES

If you really believe that God made you sick, then stop taking those "stay here" pills.

—B. B. Hankins

There are biblical laws that always work. Some non-Christians practice certain laws found in the Bible more than some Christians do, and they get certain benefits. That doesn't mean that they are going to heaven, but it does mean that they can benefit from practicing biblical laws down here.

I know a businessman who doesn't profess to be a Christian, but he is a giver. Sometimes I go by his business, and he'll give me several checks for the church. He knows that God has blessed his business. Many Christians don't even practice tithing. This unbeliever has more faith in the Bible concerning tithing and giving than many Christians do.

Any act of faith will lead you to another act of faith. Any act of obedience will lead you to another act of obedience. Frank Lloyd Wright, the famous architect, said, "What you really believe in always happens." Nothing will happen until you thoroughly and deeply believe in it. That statement is based on a biblical law. Matthew 9:29 says, "According to your faith, be it unto you."

I heard a story about a lady that had thought negatively about herself for many years. She was one of four sisters, and her sisters told her that she was unattractive. After a time, she began to believe that she was unattractive. One day a friend told her that she was beautiful. Her friend asked her what she really wanted in life, and she said that she wanted a husband, children, and a happy family. Her friend told her that she needed to paint that picture in her mind and begin to see it. She ended up having a wonderful family and a happy life.

Every person develops an estimate of himself or herself and that estimate goes far in determining what he or she becomes. You have to get a picture of what you want in your mind. You can't do more than you believe that you can. We need to get our estimate of ourselves from the Word of God.

In Acts chapter 14, there is a story about a crippled man who had never walked. This man heard Paul preach, and Paul could see that he had faith to be healed. This man really heard the Word, and it produced faith in his heart. Some people in church services listen, and others don't listen. Thirty years ago my wife was sick, and many things were going wrong in my life. I invited a missionary to come and speak at our church, and he preached for one and one-half hours. He preached about the power of Jesus and the power of faith in God. He could have talked all night and it would have been all right with me. I didn't care about time; all I wanted was God's Word. God's Word will produce faith in you. Paul told this crippled man to stand on his feet, and the man leaped up and walked. Paul "perceived" that this man had faith to be healed.

The Word of God and the Holy Spirit work together to create miracles. When the Holy Spirit works in the church, we will see some miracles. There wouldn't be so many empty hands laid on empty heads. I went to visit a sick person the other day, and I didn't lay hands on them. Why not? I perceived that they weren't ready for me to lay hands on them yet. There are other times when I perceive that people are ready, and I ask them if I can pray for them. When the Holy Spirit is working you can move beyond the natural into the supernatural.

When I minister I want to preach the Word until faith rises in people's hearts. I know that faith comes by hearing and hearing by the Word of God. As I flow in the power of the Holy Spirit, the gifts of the Spirit operate so that I know how to minister to the people who are present. As the Word and the Spirit work together, then miracles will happen.

Chapter 16

Knowing God as a Father

All people are God's creation, but not all people are God's children.

—B. B. Hankins

God is a father who loves his children. It is refreshing to see a strong father filled with strength and yet gentle and loving to his wife and children. My father disciplined me when I was a child, but I knew that he was a merciful father and that he loved me.

I remember when our family moved to the city of Wortham, Texas, in 1938 to pioneer a new church. Our nation was still in the Great Depression, which didn't end until World War II began. I also remember that our family had a very small income, and we didn't have money for school clothes. I looked for opportunities to work and make money as a child. I had a paper route, and I would find scrap metal and sell it.

When I was ten years old, I started picking cotton in the fields. I only picked about thirty-five pounds a day, but I was having a good time out in the fields. That is when they paid thirty-five cents for a hundred pounds of cotton. My dad and I picked cotton for a week and my dad said I couldn't pick cotton anymore because I wasn't picking enough to pay for my lunch. I asked him to let me try again, and the next day I went out and picked over a hundred pounds of cotton. My dad had been raised picking cotton, so he knew how to pick. He went out and picked five hundred pounds a day. It was amazing how my volume increased when I worked beside him. When there was no way for us to get school clothes, my dad went out and picked cotton to provide for us.

It's not difficult for me to have a good image of my heavenly Father. If you have a hard time seeing God as a good father because of how your father was, I believe that the Holy Spirit can give you a revelation of our heavenly Father that won't be influenced by how your earthly father was.

Jesus said that if a person loves him and keeps his commandments, then God the Father and Jesus will come and live in him (John 14:23). This is such a wonderful and majestic promise. The God who created the universe will come and make his home in me. I believe that when we let the Father live in us, a spirit of excellence will be released in us. In whatever we are doing we will do our best to honor God and bless humanity.

Jesus began the Lord's Prayer with "Our Father, who art in heaven." It is a privilege to spend time with the Father every day. I remember waking up one morning and wanting to go back to sleep, but the Holy Spirit spoke to me and asked, "You would rather sleep than talk to God Almighty?" God is the omnipotent one, but he is also my Father. It is a privilege to communicate with him as he shows us his mercy, peace, love, and truth.

Jesus prayed to the Father in John 17:23 that the world would know that God has loved us as much as he loved Jesus. It makes me feel special to know that God loves me as much as he loves Jesus. Romans 8:15 says that "we have received the spirit of adoption where we can call God Father." We have been adopted into the family and brought in legally. An adopted child is just as much a part of the family as a natural-born child.

Jesus said in John 14:9 that anyone who had seen him had seen the Father. He was saying that he was just like the Father. Do you want to know what the Father is like? Read the gospels and see Jesus, and you will know what the Father is like. Our getting to know God the Father is the key to fulfilling our purpose. There is no way to walk in the glory without some revelation of who the Father is. God the Father took all of his authority and gave it to Jesus, and then Jesus gave it to us. That truth is not worth a lot to you unless you know it and practice it.

Chapter 17

OUR PART IN GOD'S PLAN

It's not necessary unless it is necessary.

—B. B. Hankins

God's purpose for all of our lives is connected to his purposes for the previous generation. Joshua was the man who led the children of Israel into the Promised Land, but if it had not been for Moses, Joshua would not have had the opportunity. Joshua was a faithful servant to Moses for many years, and when the time came for Moses to pass from the scene, Joshua was prepared to step in and lead the children of Israel.

He led the people to fulfill the promise that God had given to them many years before. The land was promised to Abraham first. Acts chapters 10 and 11 tell the story of Peter being sent by God to Cornelius's house. The things that God calls us to do in our lives are only the fulfillment of promises that he made in generations past.

Many years ago I met a man in West Columbia known to some as the meanest man in town. This man's wife came to church, and he owned a combination grocery store and beer joint. He had a reputation as a rounder and beer joint fighter. We had weekly visitation at the church, and someone asked one of the women to go visit this man at his store. She said that she wasn't going to go because he was the meanest man in town. I started going to his store to buy some groceries, and sometimes he wouldn't even speak to me.

One Sunday he came to church and got saved. He was sixty-four years old at the time of his conversion, but in the next ten years he won more people to Christ than anyone I've ever pastored. He went after all of his old friends and brought them in. I found out that when he was a boy, as his mother was dying, she called all of her sons around her bed and said, "Boys, I want to see all of you in heaven." She prayed for every one of them on her deathbed. I was just the messenger boy who was sent to answer the prayers of his mother.

Everything we do is part of God's divine purpose, which is the redemption of humankind. Every plan and action of the Holy Spirit is for that purpose. When Peter went to Cornelius's house, he went to share the gospel message that was declared by Jesus. God's plan all along was to bring the Gentiles into the family of God, even though the church at that time was Jewish.

Cornelius was a devout Gentile who was seeking God. An angel appeared to him and told him to send for Peter who could tell him what he needed to do. Peter told Cornelius how he could be saved and filled with the Holy Spirit. Peter had been praying when God gave him a vision that changed his perspective on the Gentiles. God spoke to Peter and told him to go with two men who would take him to Cornelius's house. In Acts chapter 11, he said that the Spirit told him to go to Cornelius's house. Peter was called to preach, but God had to prepare him so that he could minister to the Gentiles.

I've known men who were greatly gifted but never could fulfill their calling because they could not change enough to minister where God wanted to send them. They couldn't change in their way of dealing with people, so they missed what God had for them. Major changes took place culturally and socially for the Jewish church to be able to reach the Gentiles.

The church always has a choice to obey or not to obey. God deals with all of our lives, and it is never easy to change. God commanded Joshua to lead the people, and Joshua had a choice. All of us have a choice to make when God gives us the opportunity to flow with him. A vision has to be birthed in every generation. It is time to reap the harvest and then Jesus will come again.

The people of our church have had to change to fulfill God's call to us as a church. God had blessed our church, but for us to go further, some things would have to change. Our church began to pray twice a day for several months, and we found out that some programs were unnecessary. We canceled a lot of programs so we could pray. The early church prayed day and night one time until an angel let Peter out of jail. If a church doesn't pray, it will not stay in the will of God.

My dad was a pastor when I was a boy right outside of Fairfield, Texas. I have gone back and talked to some of the old-timers who went to my dad's church to get some history. We talked to Sister Granberry, and she said, "Brother Hankins taught us to pray. He taught us to pray for an hour a day or as long as it took to pray through." She said that prayer is the only way that she had made it this far. A life of prayer is the only way that you and I are going to make it. We have areas in our lives that God must break through for us to be able to accomplish his will.

The first time I heard Dr. Cho was in 1977. He taught about prayer and home group ministry. Afterward I heard one pastor say that what Dr. Cho taught would work in Korea but not in America. I disagree because I believe that the Bible will work anywhere.

I have discovered the importance of the Holy Spirit in the place of prayer. In our prayer meetings the Holy Spirit would lead us to pray over different things that God wanted us to do. The Holy Spirit led us to establish elders as the spiritual leaders and the board of our church. In the Bible the terms *elder* and *pastor* are synonymous, and the elders were the pastors of the church. The pastors were the leaders, and the deacons were the servers. The shepherds were leading the sheep and not vice versa. Most American churches don't have a biblical form of church government and the deacons are leading the pastors.

My wife and I and our two associate pastors were accepted as elders in our church. Previous to accepting our pastors as elders, we had no plan of transition after I leave the scene. I've seen churches change pastors, and the new pastor will lead them in another direction for a few years. Then the new pastor leaves and is followed by another, who takes the church in another different direction.

Those churches have no stability, and they change directions every few years. No wonder churches are confused and fragmented.

I thank God for the leading of the Holy Spirit. He is the best prayer partner you can have. Jesus said that he would lead and guide us into all truth. Listening to the Holy Spirit's voice will put us in the right place at the right time.

Chapter 18

THE FAITH OF A CHILD

God has no grandsons.

—B. B. Hankins

The Bible tells us to be like children in three different places. First Corinthians 14:20 says, "In malice be children, but in understanding be men." Children don't hold malice against others. They can fight with each other, but five minutes later they are happy and have forgotten about the fight. When you get the parents involved in their child's fights, it is a different story.

In Matthew 18:3, Jesus said that unless we become like little children we would not enter the kingdom of heaven. An elderly couple was making a driving trip, and they saw a billboard advertisement for Ex-Lax that said, "Take Ex-Lax and feel young again." They stopped in the next town and bought some Ex-Lax and took it. A couple hours later the man's wife asked him if he felt any younger. He said, "No, but I just did a childish thing."

Abraham Lincoln said, "A child is the person who is going to carry on what you have started. He is going to sit where you are sitting, and when you are gone, he will attend to those things that are important. You can adopt all the policies that you want, but how they are carried out will depend on him. He will assume control of your cities, states, and nations. He will run your schools, churches, universities and corporations. The fate of humanity is in his hands."

Paul told Timothy that from a child he had known the Holy Scriptures, which are able to make us wise unto salvation. He reminded Timothy that his faith first dwelt in his grandmother, Lois, and his mother, Eunice. There are people who believe that children inherit bad traits from genetics, but I don't believe that. I believe that character comes from the environment that the child is in. The character of children comes from the training and discipline that they have received. Paul attributed Timothy's spirituality to the training that he received from his mother and grandmother.

Gifts in the hands of the untrained can be dangerous. That same gift when used by someone who is trained in the Word of God can change people's lives. When God wants something important done in the world, he doesn't change the course of nature. When he wants something important done, he doesn't send his angels. Edward McDonald said, "When God wants something important done, he sends a child into the world and puts it in a home of a godly mother who will have a dream for that child. The greatest events in the world are not battles or natural disasters. The greatest events in the world are the births of babies. Each child comes with a message that God is not discouraged with man, but he is expecting his good to be lived out in a human life." Every time you see a baby born you know that God has not given up on us yet. God said of Abraham in Genesis 18:19, "For I know him, that he will command his children and his household after him, and they shall keep the way of the Lord." Mamie G. Cole wrote a poem titled "I Am the Child." It says,

I am the child,
All the world waits for my coming,
All the earth watches with interest to see what I become.
Civilization hangs in the balance,
For what I am, the world tomorrow will be.

I am the child,
You hold in your hand my destiny,
You determine largely, whether I shall succeed or fail.

Give me, I pray you, those things that make for happiness.
Train me, I beg you,
That I may be a blessing to the world.

Every spiritual awakening in church history resulted in the establishment of training institutions to teach the principles of God's Word that were learned during that awakening. Dr. P. C. Nelson, who wrote a book called *Bible Doctrines* that I teach out of, founded Southwestern Bible College in Oklahoma and it was later moved to Waxahachie, Texas. Dr. Nelson was a Baptist minister and a highly educated linguist. He was healed and baptized with the Holy Spirit and got kicked out of the Baptist denomination. He joined the Assemblies of God denomination when it was just a few years old and then started a Bible college in 1927.

My parents started a new church in Wortham, Texas, when I was a teenager. I was the only young person in the church, and so I felt very isolated. They sent me off to Southwestern Bible College because it had a Christian high school at that time. I was only fifteen, so I know it was a tremendous emotional and financial sacrifice for them. They knew the value of investing in my life. Here at our church we have children's classes twice a week as well as bussing children in for church. Our church just approved starting a Christian school here this fall. We do these things because it is the cry of the Spirit to teach our children.

We must remember that God has no grandsons. My father was a preacher but I had to be saved just like everyone else. Some of my children had stronger spiritual leanings than others. Some of them were cold to spiritual things, and I began to pray and see God change them, and they began to be more sensitive to spiritual things. As parents you can do something about your children's spiritual desires. We can do it by prayer and training them in the Word.

The Bible says that not many wise men after the flesh are called. When the world and the devil get through with you, You are going to cry out to God for help? If we don't move with God, then God is going to move on and raise up someone else to do his will. The faith of a child is to say, "Yes, Lord, I will humble myself, and I will obey as long as I live."

Every time my mother-in-law gets her property tax statement, she says, "I don't know why I have to pay this school tax because I don't have any kids in school."

I say, "Granny, somebody paid for your kids to go to school, and now you get to pay for someone else's kids to go to school." We who are older should not lose the vision to teach, train, and stir up the gift of God in young people.

When I pastored in Flynn, Texas, an elderly man who was not yet saved began to attend the church. He had a hard heart, but one day he came to the altar and in childlike faith said, "I'm going to stay here until the Lord saves me." That old gentleman was born again that day because he came as a child. That is how all of us must come to God.

Chapter 19

Seeking God's Direction

Don't look for a word of guidance from someone else; look for confirmation from others of what God has already spoken to your heart.

—B. B. Hankins

We all need to know the mind of God concerning our decisions in life. There are times when we are at a loss to discern the right direction to take. There is a story found in 1 Samuel chapter 30 of a time when King David wanted God's direction on a decision he had to make. David asked Abiathar, the high priest, to bring him the ephod. When he brought it, David inquired of the Lord, saying, "Shall I pursue after this troop?"

And he answered him, "Pursue, for thou shalt surely overtake them and recover all." So how did King David inquire of the Lord? The ephod held the Urim and the Thummim. I'm not going to go into great detail about the Urim and the Thummim, but theologians speculate that they were a pair of flat marked stones used by the priest as sacred lots to determine the will of God. They could give a positive answer or a negative answer. David asked two questions in this passage of Scripture, and both the answers were yes.

Sometimes we miss God because we are too early or too late. One time King David asked the Lord if his troops should attack the Philistine army that was spread out before them. A prophetic word came forth that gave detailed plans far beyond what the Urim and Thummim could provide. The word said, "Don't go up, but go around to their rear and come upon them, and when you hear the sound of marching in the tops of the mulberry trees, you will know that the Lord has gone out before you to smite the Philistines." These instructions must have come from Abiathar.

That was how God gave direction under the Old Covenant, but how are we led under the New Covenant? How do we seek specific guidance today? In the New Testament we don't see any encouragement to inquire of a prophet for guidance. There were New Testament prophets who brought words of personal prophecy, but it was not sought after.

Personal prophecy has to be judged first by the Word of God and secondly to see if it confirms what God has already spoken to you. The Word can't judge some things because there are specific areas that the Word doesn't address. I'm talking about things like which workers to hire or what real estate to buy. I've had God lead me to do things that at that time I didn't know the reason why. I just knew that I should do it by the Holy Spirit.

In Acts chapter 21, a prophet named Agabus took Paul's girdle, bound his hands and feet with it, and announced that the Holy Spirit was saying that the Jews in Jerusalem would bind the man who owned this girdle and deliver him into the hands of the Gentiles. Before the word from Agabus, Paul had purposed to go to Jerusalem and after there to Rome. Acts chapter 20 says that the Holy Spirit "witnessed in every city that jail and trouble were waiting for Paul in Jerusalem." The word from Agabus didn't tell Paul not to go to Jerusalem; it just told him what was going to happen to him there.

Our primary way of getting direction from God is from the Holy Spirit and not from people. That doesn't mean we don't need godly counsel at times in our lives. Sometimes God can speak through others and open your eyes to things that you've never seen before. Through the Holy Spirit we have access to the mind of Christ. The Holy Spirit's direction is often a gentle yes or no. A yes can be a peace or a nudge, and a no can be a check in our spirit, a lack of peace, or a closed door. An open door doesn't necessarily mean that something is the will of God. Paul had open doors, and the Holy Spirit warned him not to go there.

When I first started preaching, I would go wherever I was invited to go. Once I was invited to two different churches to preach. One of them was a strong church, and I liked the pastor and wanted to go there. The other invitation was to a church in a town that I didn't like, and I didn't know the pastor there. The Holy Spirit led me to the church that I didn't want to go to. I went, and we had twelve people filled with the Holy Spirit on the first night, and the meeting lasted for three weeks.

When I pastored in East Texas, Velma and I went down to the river bottom to get some may haw berries (hawthorn berries) to make jelly. They are similar to cranberries. An elderly man went with us, and he had a fruit jar. He set it on a stump and put a haw berry on top of it. He gave me his twenty-two rifle and bet me to shoot the berry off the top of it. I took the rifle and shot that berry right off the top of the jar. That man thought I was the best shot in the county. It was just luck. That is the way I feel about the revival that happened when I preached at that church. The grace of God was on that meeting, and I just got to be a part of it.

It is important that we learn to hear and obey the Holy Spirit. When we receive no answer from God on an issue, then we should stay put. That calls for patience and trust and waiting on the Lord. I've never had any visions when I was fasting except for visions of food. I like to say that guidance from God is like cream on raw milk. It rises to the top. It will come.

There are many things that we don't need guidance on. We don't need guidance to obey the Word of God. The Word says that healing belongs to you and that God will supply your need. You don't need guidance to pray in the Holy Spirit, but you will get guidance from praying in the Holy Spirit. We don't know how to pray as we should, because of the limitations in our thinking and our knowledge.

Praying in the Spirit will also help us recognize when the answer comes. I've been healed many times by just praying in the Spirit because my spirit started affecting my body. Thank God for the work of the Spirit in all areas of our lives.

Chapter 20

Overcoming the Fear of Failure

God pays for what he orders.

—B. B. Hankins

The fear of failure is one of the biggest things that we have to deal with in life. Sometimes we don't do what God asks us to do because we are afraid that we will fail.

Oral Roberts tells the story of when God called him into the healing ministry and he said, "But Lord, what if I fail?"

God said, "Son, you have already failed, so what do you have to lose?" What does God do when he calls us to do something for him and we are afraid? He doesn't just push us out of the boat and let us swim or drown. If you pray and wait, God will talk back to you. The story of Gideon in the book of Judges is a good example.

The story tells about Gideon's conversation with God. The background of Gideon's story is that the Israelites are being oppressed by the Midianites, and God is looking for someone to lead Israel against them. So God speaks to Gideon through an angel and tells him that God is with him and calls him a "mighty man of valor." Gideon says to the angel, "If God is with us, why has all this befallen us?" In other words, "God, if you are with me, then why am I having all these problems?" Gideon goes on to ask the angel, "Where are the miracles today that God did for past generations?"

The angel responds, "Go in might and you will save Israel from the Midianites." Gideon protests that he comes from poverty and has the least ability of anyone in his family. In other words, he doesn't have any money. So Gideon goes and gathers a large army, but God tells him how to get the army down to just three hundred men. They won the battle with just those three hundred because God was on their side. If God is with you, the numbers, circumstances, and money don't matter.

I've noticed that whenever we start to build anything around here, the economy is in recession. When I first moved to West Columbia, my wife was ill, and we began to reach out for help. We went to many meetings to hear the Word and be encouraged. We were struggling for our own existence, not just to be successful pastors.

I first heard of John Osteen in the late 1950s. He was a Baptist pastor who had been baptized with the Holy Spirit. I would go to Houston to hear him speak. We attended different meetings, and Someone called us up occasionally to prophesy about God's great future plan for us. Those prophecies didn't come to pass overnight because we would go home and see that things were worse. I thought," if God wanted us here, why did we have so much trouble?"

Guest speakers would come to the church and speak about the mission of our church and the future glory of God that would be manifested here. One time Ward Chandler, a Baptist preacher who had been baptized in the Holy Spirit, came and preached a revival for us. Brother F. E. Ward got up in one of the first services and said that he saw a mighty move of the Spirit here like a great tide of water. Ward Chandler got excited because he thought that it was going to happen that week. We had a good revival, but it didn't happen that week. People would come to the church and stay awhile, but then they left because they could not see the vision that I saw. I still knew what the Holy Spirit had said would happen here.

One of my favorite Scriptures is the twenty-seventh Psalm. It is my favorite because it was the word that God gave to me when I was ill. Faith and Bobby were babies, and we had two baby beds, one on each side of our bed, so we could take care of them at night. They were only thirteen months apart, and they both had bottles. I was ill, and the devil would say to me, "Even if you survive, how will you take care of these two babies?" Fear such as I had never felt before in my life went through my veins like ice water. *I am a father, and I have four children, and things look bad.* Fear just possessed me. My wife had gone through fear before, and I didn't understand her at the time.

I didn't know a lot, but I did know that fear and faith don't mix. When faith comes, then fear has to go. That was when God gave me Psalm 27. I knew that faith comes by hearing the word, so I started talking to myself. I would ask myself if God was my light and my salvation, Then I would say, "Yes, so whom shall I fear?" Then I asked myself if God was the strength of my life. I would say, "Yes—of whom shall I be afraid?" I meditated on this verse as a prescription for my need, and the faith of God began to rise in me. My faith began to work, and I began to recover and be healed.

It is my experience that God expects some basic things from us before he blesses us. He expects faithfulness to him and his church. The great and mighty things come as we are faithful. Abraham Lincoln became one of the greatest presidents in American history, but his achievements did not come until he had experienced many personal failures. Those struggles prepared him for the battle he would face when he was president. A lesser man could not have survived what Abraham Lincoln went through, but his preparation took years.

Those who believe and continue to believe will do the will of God. The one who continues is the one who will inherit the crown. The crown is promised to the overcomer. Some people believed in me, and others didn't, but the most important thing is that God did. What God calls for and ordains moves us beyond our own desires. We can call things that "be not" as though they were, when God does it first. When something has been conceived by the Holy Spirit, it will work.

In this church we took one step at a time. We built a little porch on the front of the wood frame building that we had. Then we built a twenty-five-by-forty Sunday school addition in the back of the church. The next step was building a new forty-five-hundred-square-foot brick auditorium. Five years later we built a new brick education building. A few years later we purchased the old bowling alley from Ernest Upham, which is where we are located now. We raised $1,250 for the earnest money, and in the next three months, $12,000 came in for a down payment. When we moved down here for the first Sunday, we had a parade from one church building to the new church building.

After a few years we needed more room to minister to people and I didn't want to use twenty five percent of the church tithes that are used to operate the church to pay a mortgage. That meant we would have to cut back on ministering to people. I knew that in the Old Testament, when they built the temple, the people gave offerings that were over and above their tithe to build it. We found out about a ministry that helped churches raise money to build buildings. They had the expertise and plan to help us reach our vision. We had never done this before, but the Holy Spirit said to move forward. In three years we were ready to build, and we got an architect to design a plan to add an education wing and offices to our auditorium building. We ended up borrowing $1 million, but we paid it off with a three-year campaign of over-and-above giving. Someone asked me, "When are we going to get through building?" and I told him, "I don't think we will ever get through buying property and building." I believe that God has plans for the property we have, but he also has plans for more property around us.

I went back to Bethel where my dad and some men built a church over fifty years ago. That wood building is about to fall down now. What is more important to me than that building is meeting people that my dad led to Jesus. A building is used to touch the lives of people. That is what we are building for, to touch the lives of people.

The Bible says of King David that he "served his generation in the will of God." That is all that God requires of you and me. We are to do what God has called us to do and then pass it on to the next generation. What we do for the kingdom of God is the only thing that will last.

Chapter 21
Believing Precedes Receiving

Worry is meditating on what the devil says.

—B. B. Hankins

In Mark 11:24, Jesus taught, "Whatsoever things we desire, when we pray, believe that we receive them and we shall have them." That means that believing comes before receiving. It goes against human nature to believe that we have something before we can see it. That is why it takes faith in God.

When we ask God for a need to be met or a problem to be solved and commit it to him, there is a temptation to worry about the request before we see the answer. That is when you have to cast down reasoning and thoughts that are contrary to what you are believing God for. Thoughts will come to your mind, but you have to cast them down.

Romans 4:17 says that God calls "things that be not as though they were." We are children of God, and we are capable as well of speaking things that we believe will come to pass. I speak to myself a lot of things that I believe will come to pass. However, I don't "cast my pearls before swine." Hebrews 4:11 tells us to "labor so that we can enter into rest." I have to conceive something and get it in my spirit and then I can call those things that be not as though they were.

You will always have a battle with your mind. Peter started walking on the water, but when he looked at the wind and waves, he began to sink. If something doesn't take faith, then it doesn't take God to bring it to pass. It is just accomplishing something with natural effort. We should use good sense, but there is a cutting edge of faith. The faith principle will work in every realm. It doesn't matter if the area is family, finances, or church needs.

You can come to a place of spiritual rest. I'm not talking about indifference. Some people just give up and quit. The Bible says that those who "wait on the Lord will renew their strength." It says to "brace the feeble knees and hold up the weak hands." That is where praying for each other comes in. Sometimes people get weary, and they need someone to come alongside them and hold them up.

All Abraham did was agree with God, and that is all that confession is. You may have to speak the Word for a long time until it is birthed in your spirit. Everything in this world has to yield to God's Word. When God's Word gets in your heart, it will start coming out of your mouth.

People have asked me why I have life insurance. They don't think that you can walk in faith and have life insurance. Unless you go up in the rapture first, you are going to die someday. Our physical bodies are not designed to live forever. They asked one man if he had life insurance to take care of his family when he died, and he said, "No, when I die, I want it to be a real tragedy." We can live in faith and have life insurance for when we die of old age.

We even move in the gifts of the Holy Spirit by faith. Romans 12:6 says, "We prophesy according to the proportion of our faith." We usually operate in the gifts of the Spirit on the level of our believing. Thank God for the power of the Holy Spirit which inspires us. However, I have found that I have to walk in faith every day, whether the Holy Spirit inspires me or not. I've got to exercise my faith daily.

Jesus said in John 15:7 that if we abide in him and his Word abides in us, we would ask for what we want, and it would be done for us. I used to see that as a challenge, but now I see it as a guarantee. I know that this teaching is contrary to the world's way of thinking. If you live according to this world, you won't live according to the kingdom of God. When his Word abides in me, I will receive answers to my prayers.

Those who have believed have "entered into rest." The children of Israel couldn't enter into God's rest because of unbelief. They didn't mix faith with the Word of God so that the Word didn't profit them. I like what Hebrews 4:10 says: "He that has entered into rest has ceased from his own works." There is more faith in rest than there is in struggle and strain. There is more faith demonstrated in praise than there is in struggle and strain. You can rest in the promises of God and know that he will bring them to pass.

Chapter 22

REAL FAITH

Prayer asks and praise takes.

—B. B. Hankins

When some people see problems in the world or others' lives, they say, "Why doesn't God do something?"

God makes promises, and he fulfills them whenever those promises produce faith in people. The Bible says that God "watches over his word to perform it." God must have a surveillance system that is better than any satellite. It has been said a satellite can see a golf ball on a golf course. There is no place in this world that you can hide. God's vision is better than that, and he watches over the whole earth and searches for those who believe his word. He will respond with all the resources of heaven on behalf of one person who believes his word.

Let's look at the life of Abraham. The New Testament gives us a better glimpse at his story of faith. The best view we have of his faith is in Romans chapter 4. Abraham just believed that God would do what he said he would do. The Bible says that Abraham was "fully persuaded that God would perform what he had promised." Abraham was persuaded by the Word of God, nothing else. He kept his confidence when his faith was tested. Abraham was fully focused on God's promise in his life. Romans 4:19–21 says, "He didn't consider his body or Sarah's body. He only considered what God had said."

Abraham was one hundred years old and Sarah was ninety years old when he received the promise of a son. He continued to believe until Isaac was born. Then a few years after Isaac was born, God told Abraham to offer Isaac as a sacrifice to him. Abraham didn't waver when God told him to do that. I know that everyone has to deal with doubt in his or her life. If you get a bad medical report, it can keep you awake at night. Faith that is based on circumstances and not on the Word of God is not real faith. Real faith is based on the Word alone. To be occupied with what we see or feel is the opposite of what the Bible tells us faith is.

Do you remember the story of the brazen serpent in the Old Testament? Snakes came into the camp of the children of Israel, and many of the people were bitten and some died. They put a brass serpent on a pole and held it up, and when the people looked at the serpent, they were healed. We also must look at the promises of God instead of our symptoms.

Some people pray the problem instead of praying the answer. If you keep your eyes on problems, you will become negative about life. When my children were young, a man in our church said, "It is a terrible thing to bring children into the world today because the world is so bad." He was convinced that people couldn't raise children who would live for God. He had his eyes on evil instead of the grace of God. The Bible says, "Where sin abounds, grace does much more abound." The Word of God has to be the basis for our faith.

I think about the story of Jonah in the Old Testament. God told him to go to Nineveh and preach, but he disobeyed and got on a ship going the opposite way. He got thrown off the ship and swallowed by a whale. In Jonah chapter 2, it says that he prayed when he was in the belly of the whale. Jonah says that he "looked to God's holy temple." How could he look when he was inside a whale? He looked with eyes of faith. It is what you see in your spirit that will produce faith.

Jonah said that those who observe lying vanities forsake their own mercy. He was talking about the situation he was in. His circumstances were real and not imaginary. The whale was real, and the seaweed wrapped around him was real. Those who are overwhelmed by circumstances are forsaking the mercy of God. God never refuses to give mercy to people who ask for it. The circumstances seemed to say to Jonah that he had been "forsaken by God"; however, the Bible says, "God's mercy is everlasting." Will we look at circumstances, or will we look at God's promises? Jonah began to give a sacrifice of thanksgiving to God when he was in the belly of the whale. He was praising God in an impossible situation. I don't think that we fully grasp the importance of our praise. Jonah ended up out of the whale and walking on dry ground. He lived to write his story.

Hebrews 10:35–36 says, "Cast not away therefore your confidence, which hath great recompense of reward. For you have need of patience that after you have done the will of God, you might receive the promise." Patience is joyful endurance. Some people endure, but they aren't very joyful while they endure. Jonah rejoiced with the voice of thanksgiving. Many people don't receive the promise because they don't have patience. We have to continue to look to Jesus who is the author and finisher of our faith. We must rejoice in the Word only. It doesn't matter whether things look good or bad. Abraham was strong in faith, and he gave glory to God. That is how he received the promise, and that is how you will receive your promise.

Chapter 23

THE PSALM 1 MAN

Every promise of God is a revelation of what he wants
to do in our lives.

—B. B. Hankins

Several years ago I visited an elderly man named Sam Parten who
lived here in town. He was a contractor and continued to work
into his eighties. Whenever I dropped by to see him, he always liked
to talk about the Word of God, and I would pray for him.

One day when I was visiting Sam, he started quoting the first
Psalm, and he told me that his mother had taught him this Psalm
when he was five years old, before he had started school, and that he
had quoted it all his life. He was a living testimony of the power of
God working in a person's heart.

Psalm 1:1–3 (paraphrased) says,

> Blessed is the man who walks not in the counsel of
> the ungodly, nor stands in the way of sinners, nor sits
> in the seat of the scornful,

> But his delight is in the law of the Lord and in his law
> doth he meditate day and night,

> And he shall be like a tree planted by rivers of living water, that brings forth fruit in its season; its leaf also shall not wither; and whatsoever he does shall prosper.

The word *blessed* means happy, fortunate, prosperous, and to be envied. In the Old Testament you will read about a man doing something great, and Scripture notes that the hand of the Lord was upon him. It means that God gave him the ability to do great things. How many of you would like to be that person?

This passage of Scripture also states what that person doesn't do. He does not walk in the counsel of the ungodly or listen to their advice. Evil communication corrupts good manners. The blessed man's delight is in the law of God. He studies and meditates on it daily. Joshua 1:8 is a parallel passage of Scripture, which says, "This book of the law shall not depart out of your mouth but you shall meditate on it day and night that you may observe to do all that is written therein, for then you shall make your way prosperous and have good success."

The Psalm 1 man will be like a tree that is planted by rivers of water. In dry climates the trees are by the rivers. A tree next to the river can survive a drought because it has roots that tap into the water deep underground. In arid places you can tell where the rivers are because beautiful trees line them.

It says that "whatever he does will prosper." We've all done things that didn't prosper, and I include myself in that statement. In my case, those things didn't prosper because I didn't listen to the voice of God and follow his principles. There are principles that bring success in life. Most of those principles come from the Word of God, whether the people who teach them know it or not. You have to teach good principles to your children because they aren't going to learn them accidentally. We don't raise children for our own convenience or ease; instead, we are training them to follow the ways of God.

Jeremiah 17:7–8 says, "Blessed is the man who trusts in the Lord ... for he shall be like a tree planted by the waters and that spreads out her roots by the river and shall not see when heat cometh, but her leaf shall be green and shall not be anxious in the year of drought neither shall she cease from yielding fruit." Look at the life of Daniel. He was carried away into captivity when he was a child. Hundreds of thousands of Jews had been carried to Babylon. They were in a strange land surrounded by people who were worshipping heathen gods. The Bible says that Daniel "purposed in his heart" that he would not defile himself with the king's food and wine.

Daniel was dedicated and committed to God. The result was that God gave him favor. God gave Daniel and the other Hebrew young men knowledge and skill in all learning and wisdom. God gave Daniel understanding in interpreting visions and dreams. Our problem is not our environment but our commitment to God. Daniel was like the man in Psalm 1. He had the law of God in his heart. Daniel was in a heathen environment, but he didn't let himself become contaminated.

We also have to daily meditate on the Word of God to keep our thinking right. We are exposed to fear, doubt, and unbelief every day, but we don't have to get caught up in how the world thinks and talks. Daniel was in a heathen land, but he kept his commitment to God, and he was elevated to the third highest place of power in the kingdom. God gave him favor and honor and blessing. His enemies plotted against him, but the only fault that they could find was that he prayed three times a day to the one true God. They had him thrown in the lion's den, and the lions didn't touch him. God shut the lions' mouths so that they couldn't hurt him. If you are going through a difficult time, then just be a Psalm 1 person, and let God give you favor. Watch God bind your enemies and bring you forth.

The Bible says that Daniel prospered in the reign of Darius and in the reign of Cyrus. He prospered under both kings. God was number one in Daniel's life. If you have a lack of blessing, then look at what is number one in your life. If you will begin to be a Psalm 1 person, you will walk in the knowledge and wisdom of God. Put God's word in your heart, and it will bring you out of despair and darkness and put you on solid ground.

In Florida I met a man who was a car dealer. He said that one night he was praying and God told him to sell his business. His banker advised him against selling the business, but he did anyway. A month later the car market took a dive, and business hit rock bottom. He said that he made money, whereas if he had kept the business, he would have lost money. It pays to listen to God.

A reverence for God and his Word is the beginning of wisdom. We have to decide if we are going to do what God says or if we are going to do what man says. We can either live by what God says or live by our senses and feelings. The Bible says that God's people are destroyed by lack of knowledge. We experience failure when we don't have the necessary knowledge.

How much time do you spend meditating on the Word of God? How much time do you spend hearing the Word of God taught at church? Some Christians think that once a week is enough. If you will meditate on the Word of God, then his wisdom will become you. It won't just be what you know, but it will be you. God's wisdom won't be something that you have to reach for, but it will live in you. If you meditate on the Word, then you will always prosper.

Chapter 24

GROWTH IN THE CHURCH

We are limited by what we can't see.

—B. B. Hankins

Acts 6:7 says that "the number of the disciples multiplied in Jerusalem greatly and a great number of the priests were obedient to the faith." It says that the church "multiplied greatly." Every time you see the church grow, you can be sure that there is a reason behind it.

Before the multiplication happened, it says, "The Word of God increased." The Word of God is life, and it is alive. Jesus said that the words that he spoke were life. Have you ever read the Bible and had God talk to you just like it was a personal letter to you? Have you ever heard a sermon and thought that the preacher had been reading your mail? God knew what you needed to hear.

The Word of God increased, and then there was multiplication. I like multiplication better than addition. Faith always comes by hearing the Word. Testimonies inspire us, but God's Word brings faith. We will never grow without the Word of God in our lives and without the preaching of the Word. God gave me instructions many years ago that no matter what happens in a meeting or how long that service goes, I must not leave without presenting at least some reading or preaching of the Word.

It is the Word of God that produces our consistency. You can have experiences with God, and the devil can talk you out of them. You can't grow on experiences alone. You can't grow on just being filled with the Holy Spirit alone. The central component in spiritual growth is the Word of God. I believe in the gifts of the Holy Spirit, but the central message is Jesus.

One time a man in our church got focused on water baptism. I believe in obeying the command to be baptized in water, but I don't believe that we are saved by water baptism. He told me, "You have to be baptized in water to be right with God." I listened to him, but I didn't give in. He thought that if we could just get people baptized in water, then they wouldn't backslide. People should be baptized in water, but it is good if they are taught enough to be able to understand what water baptism is and why they are being baptized.

When you read about the growth of the early church, you see that they had some problems to overcome. They had to solve some problems that were created by revival. The move of the Holy Spirit means that spiritual babies are going to be born into the kingdom. I see the Ellison family here, and they have some problems that they didn't have a year ago. That baby has changed their lifestyle; new babies being born create good problems. When a family grows, you are going to have problems that you didn't have when the family was smaller. You can't operate a church after it is multiplied the same way that you did before it was multiplied. Don't think about the good old days when the pastor used to visit with you for three hours. You might not be able to sit in the same pew that you have sat in for twenty years.

It is beautiful to see someone accept Jesus as his or her Lord and Savior and be born again. They have been born into the kingdom of God. The same thing has to happen with the birthing of a church. Some churches are formed because some people decided that they wanted to start a church. I believe that every vibrant, thriving church has to be born of the Spirit. Most of the full gospel churches were started because there was a revival, and many people were saved and filled with the Spirit and didn't have a church to go to. It wasn't a church that was started as a split off of another church so a group of people could have their way. The churches were born by a spiritual birth.

There is a difference between a church being organized by people or being born by the Spirit. I remember when my mother lived in a community in North Central Texas after my father passed away. There were churches in the area that she had attended, but she moved to Dallas just so she could attend Oak Cliff Assembly of God where Brother Noah was pastor. She knew the growth and progress of that church, and she wanted to be a part of it. My mother's spiritual experience was in revival. She had paid a price to be filled with the Holy Spirit because she came from a mainline denomination, and her family thought that she had disgraced them when she left. My mother knew what it was like to live in the power and working of the Holy Spirit, and she wanted to be in that atmosphere.

If you were born in the fire, you still like to smell the smoke. When you are born in revival, you are not satisfied with anything else. You can't be satisfied with cold, dead religion anymore. In Acts 2:47, it says that the Lord "added to the church daily." Healthy growth is regular growth and not just an occasional growth spurt. Some churches' growth plan is to have a spring revival and a fall revival. That may be religion, but it is not the Bible, which says that the Lord added to the church daily. A church needs to be full of people with compassion for the lost so that they are winning people to Jesus all the time. Healthy people have children.

Acts 2:46 says that the people "continued daily with one accord," and that means that the church had unity. The church had a unity of the Spirit. If you aren't flexible, then you will break, so stay flexible. Our unity has to be in the fact that we are committed to reach the lost with the message of Jesus Christ together. We should be enthusiastic about Jesus. You just have to be able to tell people what Jesus has done for you. In our church services we need people that you have led to Jesus and brought with you.

The most thrilling experiences that I have are when I am involved with this church. It is a growing, living, exciting bunch of people. I never get tired of what I am doing because I am associated with people who have a vision who reach out and care. It is marvelous to see buses going out and seeing visiting teams going out. We have never let barriers keep us from going. I heard that someone said that they wouldn't mind attending our church if it wasn't so far. It is just as well that they don't come. If they don't have any more vision than a few gallons of gasoline, then they wouldn't fit in here anyway. A living, healthy, and vibrant church is just going to keep on growing and growing. I say: "Lord, look at what you are doing." The most exciting thing in the world is seeing people being won to the Lord and then ministering to their needs.

I am glad to be associated with people who have a vision. If you want to grow in your spiritual life, then tell someone what God has done for you. You will get filled with the Spirit all over again.

MESSAGES BY VELMA HANKINS

Chapter 25

THE DIFFERENT KINDS OF PRAYER

Some people think of prayer as drudgery, so they avoid it, but prayer is practicing the presence of God. Prayer is living in God's presence. It is a privilege and a joy. We need to learn how to cultivate the presence of God.

I like to pray in the secret place where I shut everything else out and pray. I don't always go to a literal prayer closet every time I need to pray, but my prayer closet is my spirit. Sometimes I pray out loud and sometimes I pray in my spirit.

Prayer is such a big subject that you could teach for years and not cover it all. Prayer is primary because it produces so many benefits in our lives. John Wesley said that God would not intervene in our lives unless someone asked him to. God gave dominion over the earth to man, and when Adam and Eve sinned, they gave dominion of the earth to Satan. Second Corinthians 4:4 says that Satan is "the god of this world." People are born into sin, and Satan is their master until they get born again and make Jesus their master.

God's will is not always done in the earth, and that is why Jesus taught us to pray for God's kingdom to come on earth as it is in heaven. If we want God's intervention in the earth, we must pray for it.

It is necessary to set aside a time daily to pray. The psalmist said that God "daily loads us with benefits." It takes time to receive our daily benefits from God. Those benefits are forgiveness of sins, healing of our bodies, divine protection, and God's love and mercy. I like to pray in the morning, but some people may find other times as best for them to pray.

My favorite prayer partner is the Holy Spirit. He is our comforter, counselor, intercessor, and advocate. I've been strengthened many times by just reading what the Bible says that the Holy Spirit does for us. He is one who is "called alongside to help us." Romans 8:26 says that he "makes intercession for us." He joins with us in prayer to change a situation. I've found that the Holy Spirit will not do my praying for me. He will help me when I pray and as I pray.

Ephesians 6:18 (NIV) says to "pray with different kinds of prayer," which means that there are many different kinds of prayer. There are different spiritual laws or rules that apply to the different kinds of prayer.

One type of prayer is the *prayer of faith*. The prayer of faith functions to change situations. Mark 11:23–24 says, "Whoever shall say unto this mountain be removed and cast into the sea and shall not doubt in his heart but shall believe that those things which he says shall come to pass, he shall have whatsoever he says. What things so ever you desire, when you pray believe that you receive them and you shall have them."

Jesus said to speak to the mountain, so this is a commanding prayer. There are mountains that we need to move out of our lives. It is not telling God about the mountain, but it is talking to the mountain.

The prayer of faith believes before it receives. Most people believe after they receive. Prayer has to be based on the will of God that is found in his Word. If you don't know what God's will is concerning an area of your life, then read the Bible until you do know what God's will is.

Another type of prayer is a *prayer of dedication and consecration*. In Luke 22:42, Jesus prayed, "not my will, but your will be done." A prayer of dedication is for situations where the will of God for what you want is not found in the Bible. So this kind of prayer usually has the added purpose of seeking direction and guidance from God. You pray a prayer of dedication until you know what God's will is. If you pray in the spirit about a situation long enough, you will know what God's will is.

The *prayer of commitment* is another type of prayer. First Peter 5:7 says, "Casting all your care upon him, because he cares for you." One of the biggest needs of Christians is to cast their cares on the Lord. We need to learn how to turn situations loose and let God take care of them. Psalm 37:5 says, "Commit your ways to God and he will bring them to pass." We can commit things to God and trust him, and he will perform what needs to be done. After I have committed a situation to God, then I thank him for the answer and refuse to worry.

The *prayer of worship* is another type of prayer. Acts 13:2 says that they "ministered to the Lord." Ministering to God is just worshipping him. David said that he blessed the Lord. We all want God to bless us, but we need to learn to bless God. Our love and worship are what blesses him. In the book of Acts, it says that the people were continually in the temple praising and blessing God. After you make a request in prayer, then the next step is praise and worship. Some people don't believe that God heard them until they see the answer. You have to see the answer in the spirit before you will see it in your hand.

United or *corporate prayer* is seen throughout the Bible. Acts 4:24 says that they "lifted up their voices to God with one accord." Then it says that "after they prayed, the place was shaken" (verse 31). When we have unity in prayer, we get results. That is why the devil fights both group prayer and unity. He knows how powerful unity among Christians is.

Another type of prayer is *intercessory prayer*. Jesus is our intercessor in heaven now. He pleads our case to the Father on our behalf. In the same way we are intercessors for others. We go to God on behalf of another person who has a need. There is no intercession without compassion. We may not feel love for someone, but if we start praying for them, then we will start feeling love for them. Jesus said to "pray for those that despitefully use you." If we bless someone with our prayers then feelings of love will come.

Compassion and sympathy are two different things. Compassion reaches out to help someone instead of just feeling sorry for them. I can intercede for people I know who have needs, but also I can be led by the Holy Spirit to intercede for others. The Holy Spirit will lay others on our hearts so we can pray for them.

I've taught on the different kinds of prayer so you will be able to use all of them. They all work in different ways to deepen our relationship with God and bring us answers. As you pray with every different kind of prayer, you will be able to see God answer many different types of needs.

Chapter 26

UNDERSTANDING THE MAN IN YOUR LIFE

There are psychological and behavioral differences between men and women. The difference between men and boys is the size of their toys. Men are more aggressive than women, and they change their minds more often than women. They aren't as sensitive to others as women are, and they are geared to overcome challenges.

Men are more competitive with each other and are more ego-driven. God gave men leadership ability and the desire to lead. That is why boys need a father to discipline them, in addition to their mother's discipline. A man needs to win and achieve to feel valuable.

Men appear strong and stable on the outside because they are taught that boys shouldn't cry. Some men can't cry or show emotions. If there is a marriage problem, it usually isn't the husband who seeks counseling or help. In his mind there is nothing wrong. Husbands tend to rate their marriages higher than wives do.

A man wants to dominate and outperform others to satisfy his ego. This can cause him to be reluctant to take the blame for failures. Men have relationships with each other built on respect rather than close friendship. Men shake hands, and women hug each other. Men will call other men close friends even though they may only talk occasionally. Men are reluctant to admit their needs or get outside help.

Women want men who are strong and tough but sensitive at the same time. Wives have high expectations for their husbands. They want them to be financial providers outside the home and then come home and provide for all of the family's needs. A wife wants to have his attention and affection and then have him do repairs for her. Men work hard all day, and then they want to come home and relax.

Society has placed an image on men as being sexual conquerors. That has caused many men to seek sexual conquests to boost their ego. Men can chase an attractive woman without having any plans for a relationship or marriage. They are satisfied to have sex with a woman without any relationship or fellowship.

Women need to have touch and love to be satisfied. That is why your husband might not say a word to you all day and then want to have sex; that is the way that he is made. A woman was made to nurture and be sensitive to the needs of the family.

Has your husband ever noticed that anyone in the family needs new clothes or shoes? Probably not. Generally, the wife is the one who sees the needs of the family and wants to meet those needs. Men think and usually don't feel, and women feel before they think.

Fighting is part of being masculine. If you've had boys, you know that they get into fights. Girls tend to fight with words, and boys fight with their bodies. Men live out their masculinity in the sports arena. They identify with the players, and they express more energy and emotion over sports than any other time.

A woman has to be subtle in the way she deals with her husband. If she wants to make her point, she can't come across as trying to take control. Come across as making a suggestion or asking them what they think. A man needs his ego boosted, and if his wife doesn't boost it, then he will find someone who will. A man needs to feel self-reliant and above the need for help. That is why men will rarely ask for help with marriage problems. He feels like he would be lowering his self in front of other people.

Most men act confident in public. They will do things in front of others that they won't do at home. A man can be sick with no one else knowing. He can be lost and he will never ask for directions. My husband would almost run out of gas before he would stop at a gas station.

We need to know the nature of men so we will know how to appeal to them. Some women want to win with their man by domination and control. Let's think about your husband for a minute. Does he lose well? For many men, losing is a disaster, and it makes them want to win the next time. When we have right attitudes, our husbands want us to help them with decisions. If you act bossy, then they don't want your opinion. When you are acting submissive, they will ask you what you think and listen to your suggestions.

Before you married your husband, you catered to him, and you should do that after you are married. When a man accepts Jesus as the Lord of his life, then God can deal with him on many issues. The Scripture says, "An unbelieving husband is sanctified by a believing wife."

Men were born to be providers, and they are proud of what they have accumulated. A man loses his self-esteem when he is not able to provide for his family. A man has to have a job and occupation to feel like a success. His work is the foundation of his ego.

Men also derive their self-worth by how they are perceived to be leaders in their home. They usually don't like to read marriage books or watch marriage videos because they are afraid that they aren't what the book says a husband should be. On the contrary, women are very interested in improving their marriage and see their relationship as being primary.

A man and woman are different, but they can love each other and live in harmony together. We need to understand that difference and act accordingly. We had better be walking in love if we are going to confront our husband about something. Sometimes a woman believes that a man is thinking like her, but he is not.

Women have the idea that they are going to change a man after they marry him. You can't love someone out of bad habits in a short period of time. We have to learn how to accept our husbands for who they are and not who we want them to be. We must accept them for who they are now. We can look forward in faith to what we want them to be, but we must accept them as they are now. We have to learn how to accept their faults.

I want you to think about ten good qualities that your husband has and write them down. Philippians chapter 4 says that "whatever is true, whatever is lovely, whatever is of a good report, then think on these things." The result of thinking on the good instead of the bad will bring peace to your minds. I want you to begin to meditate on the good qualities that your husband has instead of his faults.

Chapter 27

HARMONY IN MARRIAGE

You don't have to have a bad marriage in order to have a better marriage. It is usually those with good marriages who attend marriage seminars. Titus 2:3 says that "the older women [must] have behavior that is holy and that they not be false accusers or given to much wine." Verses 4–5 go on to say that they should "teach the younger women to be sober, to love their husbands and children, and be obedient to their husbands so that the Word of God won't be blasphemed."

We began marriage with vows to love and cherish until "death do us part." The couples that do not go to marriage seminars are often those with the most problems. When we get married, we give up our personal freedom. If you don't want to give up your personal freedom, then don't get married. A husband and wife complete each other. She makes up his lack and helps supply the missing qualities in his life. A wife fulfills her husband's emotional and sexual needs, his public needs and his private needs.

A husband and wife supplement each other and do what neither of them could do alone. If a wife sees a fault in her husband, she shouldn't go around talking to others about it. A wife talks about her husband's faults to get sympathy and get others to take her side. I'm not talking about when a wife goes to a marriage counselor, which is a different situation. Instead of criticizing her husband, she should reach out through her love for him to fulfill his needs and love him out of his faults.

Sharing marriage problems with your parents may create even more problems for you. The parents will usually take the side of their child against their in-law. Later, the wife may forgive her mate, but her parents may not be able to. It's harder for your parents to forgive your mate than it is for you to forgive your mate.

When you are emotionally involved in something, you may not have discernment. If you really want help, then don't go to someone who will sympathize with you. Many times wives run to people who they know will agree with them. You need people to show you the way out of your problems and not just tell you what you want to hear.

Many women think that they are going to have a perfect marriage, and they idealize their future husbands. After they get married, they find out their husband has some faults that need to be worked on, and they proceed to work on them. The Bible says that love covers a multitude of sins. If that is true, we don't go around exposing the faults of our husband.

If God has given you a desire for ministry and your husband is not in agreement, then wait on your ministry, and God will bring it about. It may not happen as soon as you think it should, but God may be preparing you for your future ministry by having you minister to your husband and family. Moses waited forty years for his ministry, but God opened the doors at the right time.

If we can't pass the test of the circumstances we are in right now, then how can God promote us to bigger challenges? We have to be faithful in small things before God can promote us to bigger things. If we can't be faithful as wives and mothers, then how can we minister to others?

Our first ministry is taking care of our families. The position of wife is not inferior to the position of husband, but they are two different positions. God ordained the husband as the leader of the household, and wives who refuse to follow will find themselves walking alone. That doesn't mean that you are inferior to your husband, it just means that God made him the leader.

Wives also need to compliment their husbands for the things that they are doing right. If your husband is not a Christian, you will win him to God by your unselfish devotion, loving acts, and charm. The only way to have a successful marriage is to center it on God. If a wife is out of divine order, then she can't bring her husband into divine order. If the devil can get husband and wife fighting each other, then he has already won.

If a wife wants her husband to be born again and live an overcoming life, then she needs to develop the fruit of the Spirit in her life. A wife is more sensitive than her husband and has a greater ability to hear from the Holy Spirit if she is listening. A wife doesn't have to submit to anything that would cause her to sin, but in other things she submits and follows.

Some women use religion to compensate for their unhappiness by getting involved in Christian activities and neglecting their family. I'm not talking about going to weekly worship services or having a prayer life, as the Bible commands us. I'm talking about busy activities that would be to excess. That doesn't mean that we don't have time to work in the kingdom of God, but we must put that in its rightful place. Some wives don't want the role of wife and mother. On the other side of the coin, a wife could use her family and responsibilities at home as an excuse not to go to church or to do nothing in the kingdom of God. That is wrong also.

A wife should be going to her husband as her counselor, protector, and guide. When you go to your husband with the right attitude and ask for help, God will use him to solve your problems. Many of your problems will never have to go outside your home, and no one outside the home will know that you had problems because you solved them in your home. God can even use husbands who aren't born again to help you.

Sometimes wives ask for help from someone outside their home because they have too much pride to go to their husband for help. That doesn't mean that you never have to go to a counselor, but go to someone who is going to pray for you and not talk about you.

Let your husband know that you think highly of his opinions. Husband and wife are more likely to come to the right decision together than the wife and someone else outside the home are.

Ephesians 5:33 says that "wives should reverence their husbands." That means that you respect your husband by confiding in him.

Husbands have a harder time talking about their feelings than their wives do. However, when they say something, you need to listen closely. A husband needs to have a friend and companion to talk to. Husbands want someone who understands them. If you are a friend to your husband, you will be an asset to him.

If you spent as much time in prayer for your husband as you do complaining about him, just think about what strength your home would have. Part of your prayer should be that God would change you and make you the wife you need to be. You can't change your husband by yourself; you have to let God change him. The Bible says that a wife's godly life will speak to her husband better than her words will.

A woman's fulfillment must first come from God before it can come from her husband. Plant the fruit of the Spirit in your marriage, and you will reap a harvest of love, peace, kindness, and patience.

Printed in the United States
By Bookmasters